Family Therapy

Teaching, Learning, Doing

Gerda L. Schulman, M.S., LL.D.

Associate Professor
Adelphi University
School of Social Work

Associate Professor
Hunter College
School of Social Work

UNIVERSITY
PRESS OF
AMERICA

LANHAM • NEW YORK • LONDON

Library of Congress Cataloging in Publication Data

Schulman, Gerda L.
    Family therapy.

    Bibliography: p.
    1. Family social work–Study and teaching. 2. Family
social work. I. Title.
HV697.S35   362.8'2532'07   81–40525
ISBN 0–8191–2081–2   AACR2
ISBN 0–8191–2082–0 (pbk.)

This book is dedicated
to the roots from which
I came and to the twigs
which sprang from me:
Monica and Michael

"It's not what you look at,
but the way you look at it"

Louis Malle
Film Director

"The need of reason is not
inspired by the quest for
truth but by the quest for
meaning"

Hannah Arendt

Contents

Acknowledgments and Thoughts

This book owes its conception to Dr. Joseph L. Vigilante, Dean of Adelphi University, School of Social Work, who believed that it was possible to write about the elusive process of teaching a special way of helping. He and Dr. Richard Belson of the Adelphi Faculty served as editors. To both go my profound thanks. Many others have contributed to this book: those who taught me and worked with me - my teachers and colleagues, my students, and the families who in a never ending flow enriched my practice and my teaching.

I want to especially thank two of my dearest friends: Elsa Leichter, who more than anybody else in the field influenced, taught and guided me and who added valuable comments to this book, and Edith Kriss who generously gave of her time and who with great care and unsparing patience did all the work necessary including the editing to prepare the book for publication.

Two principal considerations underlie both the content and the teaching approach chosen by me. One has to do with the fact that students who have been exposed to a belief system which is based on the underlying assumption "that an individual is the receptor of linear causal effects and hence the site of pathology"* need to be exposed to a different way of ordering data confronting them. The issue is not only one of working with a larger social unit (the family rather than the individual) but to grasp if possible through first-hand observation the family system. The focus is on the linkage of the sub-systems (individual family members) and wherever relevant the connection between the family and other systems (school, divorced spouse and families of origin, etc.), the patterns of relationship (relevant family sequences) and the family structure. The student will be alerted to such notions as the symptom as maintenance agent for the family balance, yet the

---

*Keeney, B.P. "Ecosystemic Epistemology: An Alternate Paradigm for Diagnosis" in Family Process, June 1979.

ix

therapeutic intervention is aimed to change the system in such a way that a new less costly balance can be achieved. Family balance can also be disturbed by special events which may lead to malfunctioning whether they emanate from structural changes or incidents of some magnitude, and here new ways of coping have to be introduced until a functioning balance can be achieved.

The second consideration has to do with how to enable students to exchange one lens for another, whether or not the old lens will be temporarily or permanently relegated to the attic and this indeed is the challenge existing for the teacher of family therapy at the university. The present state of affairs gives us only one semester to achieve this minor miracle. In my opinion the use of process which exposes the student to an authentic experience based on cognitive and experiential learning may open pathways to new concepts and modes of helping underlying systemic thinking without losing their humanity in the process.

Gerda L. Schulman

Foreword

George Bernard Shaw is reputed to have said those that can't do, teach. This may have been the most erroneous and hostile line ever written by a man known for his superb perception and insight, as well as for his monumental candor. Gerda Schulman would say this was his crudest hour.

The master teacher knows that to learn a subject well is to teach it. Good teaching requires rigorous, intensive, conscious and self-exposing preparation. This is what Schulman's work is like. The reader will quickly learn that Dr. Schulman invests all of her many-faceted self into her practice, as well as her teaching. Since these (practice and teaching) are inseparable, they demand the same commitment and investment.

The artistic and scientific approaches in Schulman's work are, likewise, inseparable and apparent in every chapter. She classifies, organizes, structures, hypothesizes and tests her work. She uses a blueprint and she looks for feedback in order to test her assumptions. Although she has scientific order in her work, she presents it and conducts herself with the techniques and fine orchestration befitting Bernstein with the Philharmonic. There is, after all, an art to science and a science underlying art. A clinician is a teacher, and a good teacher is a clinician. This is true not only because a good teacher has to have some of the empathy, insight and technique of a good clinician (differential diagnosis in teaching has great meaning) but also because very often the best therapeutic method for intervention is didactic in nature. Teaching is often therapy in itself. The relationship between the two, after all, has been too often minimized. This is, perhaps, because during the early days of the recognition of the relationship between the two, efforts to bring them together resulted in expectations that teachers be clinicians, totally and that clinicians be teachers, totally. What we need is some of each in each, and Schulman provides a prototype for this.

Gerda Schulman, in an exciting way, uses the classroom as an active laboratory. As she says, her demonstrations are live. She carefully plans her demonstration and she tests her hypotheses and adapts them in a subsequent analysis, and she teaches and demonstrates with tension. One can sense the vibrations in certain sections of the book. Like the healthy family, her work is continually dynamic and continually under tension, and continually productive.

Family therapy is, peculiarly, a social workers' milieu, for the social work profession has developed its methodology from the concepts of the psychosocial phenomenon; that is, the interface between people and the individual and groups, and their environments. Its methodological skills have been directed always at that fascinating inter-related energy-exchanging dyad between the people and the systems with which they interact and are a part of. The ability, therefore, learned over half a century of practice and experimentation to use simultaneously, the inner resources of the individual with the environmental resources to help in problem solution has been the central characteristic of social work theory and practice. It is inevitable that social workers dealing with the human systemic environments surrounding their clients and using these environmental conditions in combination with their own and their clients' resources, would quickly observe the dynamic potential of the family, both as a service target, and a service system. The outstanding writers on social work practice developed their practice model on the use of general systems theory as a way of bringing together the client, the target of service, the agency and the worker in a combined system in variable adaptations for providing a unique service in a unique configuration.*

Family therapy can trace its roots in the early alliances between social work and psychoanalytic psychology. With the beginning of the child guidance movement in America in the 1920's, the application of

---

*See work by Emily Mudd, Hofstein and Posner, among others.

psychoanalytic theory to the helping process was
seized by social workers in child guidance clinics
and later in family service agencies, as an idealized
instrument for working with families. Within twenty
or twenty-five years social workers and psychiatrists
were concentrating increasingly on service to families.
The Philadelphia Guidance Clinic and faculty at the
University of Pennsylvania School of Social Work were
instrumental throughout the forties' and early fifties', in identifying the family as a system, first
for diagnosis and later for treatment purposes. At
about this period, the work of Nathan Ackerman[1] rose
to the forefront of recognition among the more devi-
ant, perhaps the better word is "courageous" therapists looking for new and less restrictive modalities for intervention. One cannot help but speculate
on the degree to which Nathan Ackerman's work as a
psychiatric consultant to the Jewish Family Service
of New York for many years influenced his approach to
family therapy. (As far as I know Ackerman himself
never formally acknowledged this).

In all fairness, however, the "rediscovery" of
the importance of the family reflects a new kind of
thinking which formerly was not typical of professional social workers. This thinking is based on
the understanding of the individual within the context of the family as a living systemic organism with
its own rules and patterns. Holistic thinking of
this type focuses less on the intrapsychic conflicts
of the individual and more on the inter-personal
transactions within a family. Social work had a her-
itage of appreciation of the family as a most important environmental entity which affects the individual; even the concept of "significant others" was
known to social workers though they referred to these
people as "collaterals". Yet, when social workers,
social agencies became influenced and immersed in
psychoanalytic thinking this too became part of their
system by way of accomodation and acculturation.

Through their very early efforts to provide concrete services (money, clothing, emergency aid, as
well as counselling to families) social workers were,
early on, in an ideal position to be exposed to the
dynamic character of intra-family relationships.
They had visited families in their homes; found it
necessary to speak with fathers of children in
trouble, husbands of wives in conflict, foster parents and natural parents, as they struggled to under-

stand and fulfill complicated family role expectations of a changing, competitive society. Indeed, the social mission of social work thrust those early family workers into a complicated psycho-social milieu of intra-family relationships, which was for many who were thus exposed in the late forties' and early fifties', shockingly challenging, at times overwhelming. We had been learning the meaning of psycho-social diagnosis, but its application to families was bewildering. Families were complicated, integrally bound, ever changing. Psycho-dynamic psychology had added insights to the functioning of individuals and pairs. Its translation into family dynamics required the repeated experience of workers and psychiatrists, working together in staff meetings in the mutual assessment of problems, and on analyses of the juxtaposition of intra-psychic conflict with social conflict. Out of this mélange and the genius of a few leaders like Ackerman, Satir (and others) developed the rudimentary efforts to understand the family as a dynamic social system. The utilization of general systems theory during this period in the teaching of human behavioral phenomena to social workers was another asset. The process of the growth of family therapy as a treatment modality has snowballed in the past twenty years. Practitioners in the helping professions have been approaching it with a desert-like thirst. The technological developments of tape recorders and videotapes aided the process.

Today like all popular movements, family therapy suddenly seems to be the property of everyone, whether they are prepared or not to do the job. Dr. Schulman's work makes it clear that family therapy is a sophisticated, professional modality which can be used only if taught in conjunction with formalized, professional education in the helping disciplines. The book presumes that the student has a basic knowledge and skill in the helping processes. It is not a cookbook for the uninitiated. Her insistence on preparation, on establishing a knowledge base, on basic techniques and skills cannot be minimized. The book can be useful to the professional practitioner doing family treatment, and to those practitioners who would teach family treatment. I believe it also has special value for those responsible for curriculum development in professional schools. It is written at a point in the history of family service and family intervention which can be traced back some fifty years. It assumes that the practitioner is aware and is a product of

those fifty years of development in the helping professions. It is, in the truest sense of the word, a
clinical piece, and yet it is a teaching piece. Clinicians, teachers, thinkers and doers are welcome
here, where they belong: together.

Joseph L. Vigilante
Dean, Adelphi University
School of Social Work

REFERENCE

1. Ackerman, Nathan W., Treating the Troubled
    Family, New York:Basic Books, 1966.

CHAPTER   I

INTRODUCTION

Understanding the processes of teaching family
therapy requires an understanding of the difference
between learning through experience (practice) and
experiential learning.

Experiential learning is learning which is obtain-
ed through consciously combining affective and cognitive behavior, after the experience, not during the
experience. It is post hoc learning, whereas learning
through experience may be described as learning which
is simultaneous with the experience. The use of the
experiential teaching method helps to minimize the dichotomy between the academic work and the field work.
It is a holistic way of teaching, and aims at making
learning a total experience.

This teaching thus addresses itself to the student as a member of a group with whom he shares a common goal (learning family therapy) and to the student
as an individual who carries other roles outside the
classroom. All of this contributes to the learning
experience. It is the utilization of the sum total
of his past and present self as a member of the family of origin and his present family that the classroom and each member of the class becomes an "Instant
Laboratory". Here the experiences outside and inside
the classroom come together.

This book thus deals with a particular brand of
teaching in which the experental elements are
heightened by the teacher's conscious, deliberate and
almost constant use of the "here and now", as the student experiences the class. This is done through
highlighting transactions occurring in the classroom,
reactions of the class and the connections between
these incidents and family therapy. The use of structure and process is the constant thread by which this

is accomplished. The class (a group) is gathered to achieve certain group goals, as well as goals for each individual. It is _time_ _limited_: a fact which has profound impact on both the students and the teacher. Therefore, the experiential learning process is characterized (like life) by a Beginning, a Middle, and an End. Equally, the structure has a hierarchical component which impacts on the process. The teacher is in a certain power position and the students have lesser status while, at the same time, all are totally interdependent.

While any group consists of individual members who bring to it experiences from their past and present life, the fact that this group is a class creates a special and immediate pressure to learn cooperatively. The primary focus in the class is to elicit the universal thoughts, feelings and problems created not just by one but by several experiences, to encourage the group to find alternate possibilities and for the teacher to extricate the basic concepts governing the group's thinking.

Because of my conviction that the quality of actuality and "aliveness" is essential for experiential learning I do not use "canned" case material (that provided by people outside the classroom). The case material is brought by the students themselves. I use examples from my own practice and class transactions to illustrate and make alive certain points and issues. The only exception is when I introduce video tapes by well-known family therapists who either dramatize aspects of my approach or who use methods quite different from mine.*

After some early resistance, the climate in the class becomes one of readiness to look at themes and patterns which have to do with "everyman's" family: the position of an only child, of a late born, one of many children, a child of divorced parents, and so on. The aim of these discussions is not as is sometimes feared, to get students to share prematurely what his or her family was like. The purpose is, rather, to

---

*We are currently using tapes by Dr. Salvador Minuchin, emphasizing the structural approach, Peggy Papp's Family Choreography, and Virginia Satir's "Family in a Crisis" demonstrating the so-called growth model.

stimulate thinking by playing out of certain family scenes or typical family features and to demonstrate the influence all this has on family transactions and attitudes. However, it often occurs that memories with highly personalized feelings are touched off.

In my teaching, work with the group is given preference over work with the individual. Similarly, the whole family unit takes priority over the sub-group or the individual (at least in the beginning phase of treatment.) This is often experienced by students as a dramatic difference from what they have learned so far. Students (not unlike some members in a family) may feel neglected, lost, and confused. Others feel relieved by this focus and have a remarkable ability to extricate what is germane for them. Always, there is an attempt to balance the needs of the group with the needs of the individual not so much to be "fair" but to be ever alert to what goes on in the group and by making overt what is beneath some of the rationales for behavior offered by the group. There is a continuous sharing of what prompts my moves in the process. This replicates what I do with families (on occasion), but with students it is done consistently.

Underlying this approach is my belief that for optimal learning the class needs to first become a group in order to enlarge the field of interaction so that learning and interpersonal growth can take place. The dialogue which is influenced by the hierarchical structure, and therefore tends to be teacher centered, needs to be widened to increase interaction. I deal with the class similarly to the way I work with families by trying to modify certain "group"patterns rather than to initially focus on the individual. Thus I identify some students' tendency to sit back and let others, or the leader, carry the ball before moving to feelings like fear of exposure, or competitiveness. This process serves as a model for the student in his own work with families. Eventually, as in families, the class moves from the general to the specific, from the group to the individual, from generalization to differentiation. In the ending phase, the "whole" takes priority again through mutual sharing of the profound experience of ending which, whatever the individual pattern, is shared by all. In most instances at this point, the individual students have already reached a level of autonomy; they have been able to empathize with what is universal. This is the goal for a successful class, as with a family which has grown.

3

Since, however, this book is not only a book about a teaching method but about the teaching of a certain "modality" which is based on systemic thinking, there is considerable discussion of family therapy itself: classification of family types, predominant family quality or characteristics (family features), developmental stages, and relationship of the presenting problem to the family system, how intervention is determined. Content, however, will rarely be taught "pure". It will be interwoven with process and address itself to the student in his various roles and functions: as a member of the class, his family and as a family therapist. There is also a discussion of student types, the mix of teacher-student, and its effect on the class as seen by the instructor, and by the students. I have tried to convey a quality of teaching which defies adequate description. It is like the conductor of an orchestra, who is able to evoke a vital response from the musicians, which in its totality, both surpasses and intensifies the work of the individuals. With each new class I experience anxiety, curiosity, excitement and an intense trust in what is bound to happen and always does when someone with some knowledge and sensitivity exposes himself to a group of people who want to take in, and give out, to learn and teach, to think and do; who are beset by their own feelings and expectations, wishes and fears, and are bound together by a common purpose. What emerges is like a symphony, atonal at times, harmonious at moments, but always forming its own distinct quality of sound.

CHAPTER II

BEGINNING: THE FIRST CLASS

A first encounter can begin a relationship which
will be influenced by the quality of the encounter itself. A teacher should not underestimate the profound impact of this first encounter which goes beyond the superficial first impressions which are formed. The deliberate use of the interpersonal dynamics,
inherent in the first class, leads to the formation of
a group which, in turn, becomes a laboratory for learning. I am not sure when a beginning actually starts.
Does it start at the moment when the topic is introduced, when the first important question is asked or
answered, or when the class shows the first indications of working together? Or, does it already exist
as phantasies of the participants preceding the initial experience. For one, it may be the expectation
of a special course or teacher; for another an an-
noyed, burdened feeling that yet another course has to
be taken; for other students, a vague malaise symbol-
izing trusting or excitement. The instructor, like
the student, is subject to a multitude of feelings
about the coming encounter. I most commonly feel
pleasure, coupled with some anxiety about meeting a
group of strangers and some awe as to what is going to
happen.

The first minutes before the class starts are
filled with tensions which get expressed in various
ways, like mutually looking each other over, hustle
and bustle of excitement approaching chaos; there is
a tendency for some to cling together (sub-groups with
a shared past). Others sit apart and occupy themselves with "busy work", while a few, possibly in response to my unintended signals, try to make contact
with me - something which is, in part welcomed and in
part, felt as a disturbance. I struggle to deal at
each first class with my own feelings and thoughts.
Throughout, I am trying to be open to what develops in

5

this pre-group phase of the class. I have often
thought that it may be easier to enter the room precisely at the appointed hour, hoping that by then
most students would have settled down. Yet I don't
like to miss (or protect myself from) the initial encounter.

Phantasies and expectations are important factors
influencing the class. So is my insistence on physical structure. We sit in a circle. I am prepared to
go through a considerable amount of trouble to
achieve this. There seems to be a stubborn counter-
force in academia where the instructor, as the priest
in church, is elevated or at least centered before
rows of students with no way of looking at each other.
They are forced to look at the instructor as the head.
One of my first"activities"is my pushing seats into a
circle. Always some students help. In addition to
the welcome relief I get from the discharge of anxiety and the active contact with some students similarly engaged, the message is transmitted[1]: "In this
class we will be people, not simply students and instructor; we will look for stimulation from each
other; we will pay attention to verbal and non-verbal
messages, and we will strive for some intimacy".

Finally, the time to start has arrived and the
plunge has to be taken. I might address myself to
the group's behavior. It might be to "the look" on
the part of the students - "all eyes are upon me and
the mouths are open", which I liken to how some families initially act with the therapist. The group is
encouraged to speculate at the meaning of such behavior
and the temptation for the family therapist to respond
to it and become "the feeder". As an alternative to
this tendency I propose to stimulate family interaction so that the family cannot only "learn about itself" by becoming more aware of their transaction but
can look for some solutions. For example: instead of
immediately answering a family's question as to the
purpose of the family session, one might direct the
parents to answer the children. Or if there is total
immobilization, the family therapist may talk about
"everybody's hard time to risk". In relation to this
phenomenon which was identified by the students, I
might talk about characteristics existing in some families, e.g. "the helpless parent phenomenon" who
wants magic from the therapist. If the family therapist (like the instructor) is flattered by the "omnipotent" role, he will tend to oblige and overlook the

potential in the family to do things for themselves.
Or the therapist, especially if he is inexperienced,
may be frightened by the expectation that he should
have "all the answers" and would naturally feel helpless, do too much for this very reason. While feelings like these may also occur in the experienced family therapist, he has so many "tricks" at hand that
his malaise tends to be covered up. When this is made
overt and likened to the instructor's feeling at the
beginning students feel reassured in knowing that the
"omnipotent" teacher can be as uneasy as they.

At other times, if no opener exists, it is helpful to get some sense from the students regarding
their expectations, their hopes, their wishes, and
their fears about the class. I ask about their practice, field work or internship: where they are working and what practice questions they are struggling
with. Responses tend to be both spoken and expressed
in behavior. I use this opportunity to emphasize the
importance of the non-verbal communication. By ad-
dressing the questioner as a possible spokesman for
others, the one who takes a chance while others sit
back, demonstrates that the group gets priority over
the individual. I am also calling attention to different ways of dealing with a new situation - "some
are guarded and some are not". Students often respond to my comments by giving "reasons" for their behavior, reasons which reflect their value system and
the causality of their thinking. Those who have spoken may explain that "they always do it" and/or are
"driven by anxiety". Others apologize for holding
back with the explanations like they fear that their
questions might be considered "primitive or naive".
A wealth of expression and thoughts of varied coping
patterns flow from underlying feelings which range
from a need to comply to "mom's" request to the fear
to outshine or disappoint one's parents and siblings.

At this stage it is important to convey as light-
ly as possible that "anything goes" and all is acceptable and useful. I emphasize that none of my comments
mean disapproval but are intended to enhance the process. However, I show least interest in "because" explanations, but show preference for what is and what
is happening among us as well as the timing and context of comments.

When I discuss my relative disinterest in "causes"
students either do not believe me or are critical

7

since my statement runs counter to mechanistic theories of cause and effect with which they are imbued.
They need to understand that most syndromes are caused
by the convergence of many causes which, like the uni-
verse, are in constant motion, but governed by recur-
ring patterns! This provides good opportunity to make
a point about families as systems. I am not asking
the student to swallow what I say, but to hear and
respond. Yet I try to make my point of view as a family therapist clear: behavioral messages are as important and often more telling than verbal statements;
social and family roles and patterns of behavior are
centrally significant. Often my approach in the beginning creates a certain self-consciousness as we talk
about so many things which traditionally are not talked about in class. I try to balance the self-consciousness by certain "lightness" in my behavior. For
example my response to a student's complaint that my
calling attention to this or that takes his* sponta-
neity away simply was, "So, you don't like what I do".
Then I move on.

Sometimes a specific "incident" can be used to engage the class rapidly. Once, several minutes prior
to the first class, which was filled to capacity,
some students who were not registered asked permission
to join. Our discussion became somewhat agitated and
did not lead to a satisfactory solution. The interaction was noisy and took place in full view of the
other students. I asked the class whether they had
noticed what had gone on between the group and myself.
It was surprising to me to learn that none had noticed
anything. I compared this phenomenon to "open family
secrets", stressing how some children learn to stay
out of fights between their parents and how this can
be followed by successful "tuning out" to such a degree that many disconnect themselves from (real) family events. It was then that students acknowledged
that they had indeed noticed a conflagration. They
thought it best not to get involved and actually had
"forgotten" about it. Some students were uneasy about
the struggle, especially since it involved an "authority figure"; some perceived me as "in trouble and
helpless", others did not want "to take sides". I was
delighted at how quickly we had dealt with important

---

*Although the student is referred to as "he" it may
also be applied to the female student.

8

issues occurring in many families. We had been in
touch with our individual feelings about it, and we
could see how different people had different reactions
and different coping patterns. The class behavior was
compared to a family consisting of a parental person
and lots of "children"; the latter were divided in a
pro-parent and in a pro-sibling group, yet all had decided not to mix and then had acted as if nothing had
happened. I observed that if I hadn't talked about
it, some of the feelings may have gone underground and
may have affected our later proceedings. As family
therapists, they would witness comparable incidents in
families.

It became clear that most students were now interested, some a little scared, others just puzzled.
After commenting on this, I presented to the class the
dilemma - should I accept several additional students.
By now not much prodding was necessary. Some students
were for letting them in, others were against it because of the size of the class and the sacrifices they
would have to make, and others were (you guessed it)
clearly on the fence. As the discussion went on various students changed their point of view, several especially after one of the outsiders said angrily that
if the whole thing was such a hassle she preferred to
leave. It was time to intervene as the leader. I
stated that I was not asking the class to make a decision for me. The decision, however, was in part
based on the class members' thoughts and feelings.
Responding to the angry student, I said that I heard
her anger and was not surprised since I had put the
group and her into a difficult position. I furthermore
assumed that the angry student probably expressed what
most of the out-group was feeling. I asked them for a
bit more patience since, whatever the outcome, it would
help us all to understand process if we worked this
out together. I admitted to feeling uneasy and somewhat guilty myself for "dramatizing" such an incident.
It also reminded the out-group that they too carried
some responsibility because of their refusal to take
"no" for an answer. Thus, we all shared responsibility
for the "crisis". Both sides of the class had expressed human feelings which I too shared. If I accepted the outsiders, there would be some who would
feel I had deprived them. If I excluded them, then
others would see me as rigid and ungiving. It just
meant that all actions have consequences, rather than
that they are "right" or "wrong". I make this point
with families in treatment who are governed by a

strong sense of morality. I became silent, and the group (the ins and the outs) began to talk to each other. They listened, they responded, they changed positions and one of the "out-students" sadly said that she knows now what she would miss if she had to leave the learning situation. When it became obvious that the class too could not make a decision, I decided against enlarging the class. (Note: I did not say "against accepting the out-group.") I let them know that I had heard what each one felt and, in a way, I shared their feelings including some dislike for my own decision, but that I was prepared to bear the consequences - their anger and disappointment. The students left - some sad, some angry and some relieved. Two of them came to a seminar I gave at a later time; one sent me a message about the meaning of this experience.

The subsequent class discussion provided me with a further opportunity to help them understand the authority of parental figures in a family (to make ultimate decisions about survival or boundaries of the family). Yet while this is generally accepted in organized families where parents have been able to carry parental functions, there is a pervasive fear that letting children express their thoughts and feelings reduces rather than enhances parents' ability to make the final decision. This led to a spontaenous discussion in the class as to how often parents do not tell their children about things they assume the children will not like. Parents may fear that they either will then change their position or they are uneasy to hear children reflect their own inarticulated doubt. Examples of families dealing with death and divorce were given by the students. Some students began to see patterns; some had been "identified" with me and others with their peers. This discussion led to some recognition that often a person's original position in his own family affected behavior even in regard to innocuous situations as the one we all had experienced.

Towards the end of the first class session, I try to spend some time in defining my own expectations. However, because of the experience we have shared. a common frame of reference has developed and words have already taken on special meaning. The students have some sense of how I operate, my style, and even some of my idiosyncrasies. In short, they have had a taste of the kind of teaching I propose

to engage in, with its inherent expectation that they
will have to take some initiative in the learning process. They will have to take responsibility by letting me know when I go too fast, am unclear, or repetitive since I am not a mind reader. The student will
have to do a great deal of integrating on his own.
This will largely depend on how much involvement they
will allow themselves as individuals and as a group.
I point out that I consider us to be a working group,
a laboratory in which our interaction will be an important tool which will be used to understand ourselves as members of the group, as members of our own
family and form the necessary base to become family
therapists.

Students are expected to bring to class their experiences as practitioners which include or will lead
to work with families. Those students who will not be
working with families will be at a disadvantage. Although graduate students are not independent practitioners, I suggest that like family systems influence
and circumscribe individual systems, individuals, especially if supported by outer systems, can influence
the family (agency). It has never ceased to surprise
me how many students who were placed in agencies with
strong individual treatment orientation have found
ways to have sufficient impact on the agency to be
permitted to work with families.

While beginning with the whole family is - to my
mind - the most appropriate way of entering the system, beginning with individuals and eventually moving
to the whole, will give to the class an opportunity
to experience a different way of family engagement. It
dramatizes the type of resistance occurring after a
dyadic coalition - therapist and client - has been
established and what happens to the newcomers as well
as those who make up the original team when the
field becomes enlarged.

Usually, in the first class session, sometimes
later, I comment on the specific structural characteristics of our group which, I assume, will have
meaning for our future together. I refer to the uneven distribution of gender - more often than not
there are few and on occasion only a single male student. There is usually an uneven distribution of mi-
norities - most of them blacks or Puerto Ricans - in
contrast to the outside world where they are more
heavily represented. When there are older students

11

it is mentioned. The purpose is twofold: comments
on structural singularities emphasize that structure
leads to a certain organization. Sometimes sub-groups
are formed reflecting the human tendency to cling to
the familiar. Often, unfortunately, this leads to separation and alienation.

Since "being the only one" or "just a few" is
bound to evoke feelings, the recognition of the existence of different groups decreases the taboo which
tends to exist. The taboo contains the message:
"Let's not talk about it." It is almost as if the
most visible element, the one which is an external
characteristic (age, gender, physical handicap, race)
is least likely to be talked about. Most of us were
raised with the powerful injunction that it isn't
nice to notice physical characteristics of people as
if the fact of the noticing of such characteristics
in and of itself were embarrassing. This tendency
may, in extreme cases, lead to "not seeing" which in
turn implies that what "is, is not". This taboo is
shared by the mental health profession which, while
ready to talk about people's inner feelings and phantasies, seems reluctant to focus on external facts -
behavior or the way a person looks. While such attitude may make sense within the framework of the individual psychoanalytically oriented approach in which
the therapist waits for the patient to initiate his
concerns and because of a tendency of analytically
oriented professionals to minimize the externals, the
family therapist who deals with behavioral and transactional characteristics and patterns needs to be
ready to deal with these unmentionables. After the
class has brought out some feelings in relation to all
this, I make a connection from our group to families
who rarely allow themselves to talk about such obvious syndromes as e.g. a woman's feelings of loneliness because she is the only female in the family;
the one member of the family who looks strikingly
dissimilar from others. So it goes for many other
differences - stature, color, race; the more deli-
cate to handle because societal attitudes have often
discriminated against different groups, making the
label itself criticism.

Therapists coming from the same milieu are, of
course, bound by the same taboos as their clients.
Hence so-called sensitive therapists may avoid talking about the fact that a family is black and its relevance to the situation. They fear they shall

appear prejudiced. The implication is that noticing
and talking about difference implies something negative! Like other essential areas, this issue - the
importance of structure needs to be worked at consistently. While I have made considerable headway in enabling class groups to be freer around many charged
subjects, I have been least successful when it comes
to an open exchange regarding racial differences.

I consider it essential somewhere before the end
of the class to pause and give the students a chance
to express their reactions. If I am ready to really
hear and receive, important messages tend to come out
which build the bridge to the next class session.

REFERENCE

1. Schulman, G.L., "Teaching Family Therapy to So-
    cial Work Students" in Social Casework, July 1976.

CHAPTER III

IS TEACHING FAMILY THERAPY DIFFERENT?

Is Teaching Family Therapy different from teaching other clinical subjects? It seems to me that the task of the person who teaches Family Therapy is to utilize the simple fact that all students have a personal knowledge of families. All were born into families and are, in one way or another, involved with their families of origin. If they have established new family units these also provide a first hand resource. Some of the knowledge emanating from these experiences is readily available; other knowledge potentially exists as it is hidden behind emotions which affect one's objectivity. Yet this very fact makes discussion about families richer and more meaningful. The teacher must enable students to separate facts from feelings so that both components can be integrated eventually, and lead to clearer perception.

Several methods have been developed to facilitate this process: sculpting one's own family, genograms, eco-charts, the playing out of important family scenes, phantasy exercises like the "imagining that one's own family - either then or now - would enter family therapy", etc. Some training endeavors make a point to begin with working on the student's own family rather than focusing on clients' families. Whatever techniques are used, most assume that within all of us is a rich reservoir of knowledge about the family. This kind of teaching arouses some anxiety and may account for some initial resistance. Another factor which may account for a certain hesitation on the part of the students to learn the family approach may be related to earlier exposure to ego psychology with its focus on the individual and its emphasis on transference.

The Family Therapy instructor in his teaching takes it for granted that the student has some know-

ledge of individual psychodynamics and developmental
stages. This is necessary for understanding the individual within the family group and for the later
working through phase with the frequent focus on
pairs and individuals. The individual can be better
understood, of course, when seen in the complex situation of his family.

If in the future family study and treatment will
precede the teaching of ego psychology, family therapy teachers may have to follow a different sequence.
However, at present students need to be helped to
move from the individually oriented framework into a
holistic one; to focus on transactions between dyads
and to understand the system within which all actions
and transactions take place.

As I have indicated, my approach is holistic-
systemic, experiential, group related and it synthe-
sizes the cognitive with the "feeling-doing" aspect.
Thus teaching flows from the here and now of the situation (class); it depemds on structural phenomena
and it takes place within the context of time. Facts
are never presented "in a vacuum", but these emerge
and are constantly interwoven. The selection as to
what to deal with first - an ever-vexing problem especially for beginners in the treatment of families
- may be the crux of the matter. No matter whether
the focus is first on the transactions between students and myself, students among themselves, the student as a member of his own family, or the group process (feelings and behavior re beginning, for instance), parallels or differences between what occurs
here and what may happen in families are constantly
drawn. Issues, such as, do we address ourselves to
the need of one person versus the need of the group,
do we deal with the overt plea or deal with the underlying are the threads which form much of the content
of class learning. Throughout, the emphasis is not
on a "right or wrong way" but to contemplate together the possible consequences of one move versus
another.

This kind of process is not orderly - it touches,
confuses, brings forth reactions, associations - yet
there is a thread of connectedness from the very beginning. While there are great similarities to what
may occur in initial family work, there is in the
teaching situation a consistent effort to extra-
polate the concepts, usually after they occur. Thus

16

the instructor-teacher as the leader responds, facilitates and theorizes. It is as if she*walks a tight-
rope between the fine line of therapy and teaching
and indeed there are moments in every class in which
this question comes up; as do the questions whether
group or individual needs are more important, should
learning-teaching be more cognitive-theoretical or
more experiential? The point I wish to make is less
that there is an either/or but that the teacher by
introducing the "otherness", the "what is missing" in
the process and/or in the group at a given moment will
establish some balance between the feuding forces until such moment when the balance, as in a growing organism, is again thrown. Hence in the academic setting which is predominantly theory oriented, I stress
deliberately the experiential - the feeling and the
doing which leads to the knowing. Similarly, I am
encouraging the individual oriented class, the one pre-
occupied with the past and the causative orientation,
to stay with the whole, the present and the description of the phenomenon rather than the speculation of
the hypothetical causes. I stress the need to use
our senses more - our eyes, our ears, our sense of
touch. Yet I would do the opposite with groups -
which never happened in the classroom but sometimes
in workshops - which are only geared to feelings, to
experiencing - here I would stress the observation of
transactional facts, the use of theory, remind them
of the contract which is not to have a sensitivity
group but a group assembled to learn to treat families.

My thinking is governed by the concept which I
introduce consistently in my teaching, that after assessing the family system (through observation, exploration and engagement) the therapist needs to provide what the system is lacking. For example, the
chaotic family needs to be helped to become organized,
the overorganized family needs to find ways to become
more fluid, and the enmeshed family needs to learn to
form boundaries.

Thus, while I have stressed that I am not teaching an orderly course in which there is a prepared
syllabus for every class session, various points
which I will briefly describe are conveyed and will,

---

*"she" or "he"

it is hoped, be integrated gradually. These points
are directed to the beginning family therapist who
while engaging a family needs to assess the family
system. The timing of and the context within which
these points are being brought up depend on the
"life" of a particular class.

a) MOVE FROM THE OBSERVABLE TO THE Inferential or
   DO NOT HYPOTHESIZE PREMATURELY

Does it sound as if I instruct students not to be
creative? This is not my intention; what I mean is
that I caution students not to jump to conclusions on
the basis of flimsy evidence or to lean too strongly
on psychiatric lingo which tends to restrict a person's view. Even if such conclusions are not shared
with the family they tend to put blinders on our
senses. Instead, I suggest that students observe
interpersonal transactions and be clear whether they
occur between dyads, triads or the whole family and
pay attention to important cyclical family sequences.
I emphasize the context within which a certain transaction occurs which includes time and place and certain configurations; the significance of spontaneous
occurrences or those in response to interventions are
also stressed.

To give an example: one student described a hos-
tile-dependent relationship between a mother and an
adolescent daughter in the family. To strengthen her
point she called the daughter's provocative behavior
"masochistic" since in the student's view the daughter invited her mother's threats. The student quoted
extensively from psychological tests which confirmed
the girl's masochism. I asked the student to describe a transaction in the family which would make
her point more alive and in the process we learned
that the maternal grandmother was present in the session since she lived in the home. As per usual the
mother reprimanded the daughter for her irresponsible
behavior - her lack of helpfulness, keeping late hours,
and the like. Whenever the mother ran out of accusa-
tions the daughter flippantly taunted the mother with
her sexually tinged adventures. I wondered what the
grandmother was doing while all this went on. The
student recalled that on various occasions the grandmother had smiled indulgently at the mother's repri-
mands and at one point had offered the girl a cigarette moments after the mother had complained about

the daughter's incessant smoking.

Several students acknowledged the cyclical destructive nature of the mother-daughter relationship which the student had tried to explain in a causal way. She had mentioned that the mother had always rejected the daughter because she reminded her of her divorced husband. The student herself, however, picked up that the grandmother's action seemed to indicate a coalition with the granddaughter. Intrigued by this thought she began to speculate as to the "why" of this, a move which I discouraged. I confirmed, however, that the grandmother indeed seemed to fan the mother-daughter hostility by aligning herself with the girl against the mother, that she acted albeit in a covert way as a troublemaker. I asked the students what they thought of the mother's accepting her mother's sabotaging role. The student then remembered that the mother had turned in great anger against the daughter after the latter had accepted the cigarette, something which surprised her since the girl for once had not provoked the mother. The class was able to speculate on the basis of the above that, at least in part, the girl was the target of her mother's unexpressed anger against her mother and they concluded that treatment would be more effective if the transactions on the part of the grandmother could be altered.

In another class discussion a student referred to a father in a family as a tyrant on the basis of information given by all family members and the father himself. He tried to justify his position by calling his wife a "softie", The student was concerned because she found it difficult to relate to this "rigid compulsive man". She called this difficulty countertransference. This family came to class for an observed session. The father acted true to form, but I noted that he sat apart from his wife and children, who formed a cluster. When the father made some of his powerful statements, mother and children exchanged glances and began to giggle. The more this occurred the sterner the father became. In our subsequent class discussion the students recognized that the father's autocratic behavior was due, in part, to his being hopelessly outnumbered by the rest of the family, that he was not in a power position though he tried to act powerfully. It was also evident that the mother and the children were in cahoots and that she did her share in setting them up against their

father with the consequence that his anger was turned
against the children. This preserved the mother's
position as the saving angel, but prevented the father from working out his relationship with his children and with his wife!

Who does what - when?

Students are alerted to pay attention to the roles
of family members, their positions and the timing and
direction of their actions. The latter includes the
type of communication among sub-groups as well as the
one used by the whole family; the importance of the
non-verbal message and the position of the non-doer
is stressed and seen as particularly powerful inasmuch as it often defines the parameter of the actions
of the doers. Related to this is the role of the absent member. As students begin to cite incidents and
give examples usually stressing pathology of the individual or symptomatic behavior, I express my interest in what kind of family it is and ask them to
describe it. Is the family lively, frozen, are they
yellers, doers, can they sit still, are the children
well behaved or are they divided between the "bad"
and "good" ones? Is the division between genders,
age groups and siblings or does it cross the generational line? All these considerations lead to the
concept of family polarization. The split between
two often opposing characteristics which are carried
by different family members - or sometimes by the family outsider like the divorced spouse who represents
all the badness in the family. The link between this
concept seen in interpersonal terms and the intra-
psychic concept of ambivalence can be made here. In
interpersonal terms one part of the feeling is de-
posited onto another person, thus "freeing" the person from dealing with an inner conflict. We encounter frequently the rage of a "stuck" and "captive"
mother against her "carefree" ex-husband, unaware of
her own longings for some freedom. To illustrate
this point I may give an example of a family session
in which both ex-spouses and their children were present. In it the "envied" ex-husband talked about his
loneliness and expressed sadness that his children
were becoming strangers to him. Thus his assumed
privileged position was seen in more realistic terms.
This enabled him to consider his former wife's lack
of "freedom" which he had seen as selfishness and to
work out some sharing of responsibility for the chil-

dren to give the harrassed mother some respite from
her daily responsibilities.

While these feelings based on faulty or partial
perception are often known to the worker-therapist
and may be dealt with in individual sessions the advantages to have them expressed in front of the family not only tend to correct the perception but
create an atmosphere in which corrective actions can
be initiated.

Other feelings may be quite hidden to a person
herself and resistance against teasing them out exists even in individual sessions. With the family
present these repressed or denied feelings can be
dealt with inter-personally through encouraging
people to listen to each other and maybe even learn
from each other: the yeller may learn from the silent
one, the feeler from the doer, and the"over-conscien-
tious" one from the one who is an expert in "playing".
The latter occurred in a black family which was divided between the dutiful (good) ones and those who got
into trouble (bad). Righteousness was invested in
the mother and two daughters who were hardworking, polite and oh! so serious. The troublemaker was an adolescent daughter whose mischievous eyes gleamed when
she described her escapades which bordered but just
avoided delinquent behavior. In the family she had
the unenviable role to remind everybody of the father
who had been kicked out by the mother because of his
incessant "playing" (he was a gambler). I shared with
the class that when listening to the endless accounts
of virtuousness I had an irresistible urge to become
"naughty" and to "tease" and I wondered whether Leslie,
the "bad" 16-year old one, may be plagued by similar
impulses. It turned out that the split was not only
carried by Leslie, but had been an issue several
years ago when the now 20-year old daughter, Irene,
was in mid-adolescence and returned home from an out-
ing very late. In a rage the mother "expelled" her
for two months during which time she went to live
with an aunt until the remorseful girl was permitted
to return and never was "bad" again. I labelled this
family as being very fortunate since they had developed such expertise in two important areas: duty and
responsibility, and the knowledge how to have fun. I
gave the task that each expert was to teach the other
- Leslie was to teach Irene and her younger sister
Joanie, how to enjoy themselves, and Irene needed to
teach Leslie how to be responsible. In the following

session, after the girls talked how they had handled the assignment, the mother began to talk about her yearning for freedom and wish to have more time for herself.

b) MOVE FROM MORE TO LESS

The holistic point of view emphasizes interdependence of sub- and related systems and trends to move from the greater unit, the family, to the individual. If for one reason or another one needs to deal with an individual, deal with his role in the family, consider the possibility that he may be the SPOKESMAN for others (again do not jump to conclusions but test it out) or deal with his position: he may be a BALANCER or PEACEMAKER for the family or the one who expresses a hidden quality. The acting-out child in a life-less, depressed or too static family operates, albeit in exaggerated ways, as a life force, the bringer of excitement and even joy. Comments like "in your family everybody seems to be frozen except Johnny, who can't sit still" may highlight this. Seen from another point of view it shows how a family deals with differences - do they indulgently smile at the antics of a child, or reprimand him, expel him, threaten him - do all family members act and feel the same way or are there some subtle or open coalitions, double messages, etc. Thus, attention has to be paid to the family transactions in regard to one person rather than focusing on the person per se.

This need not be taken as an absolute rule and it will depend on the purpose of a particular intervention E.g., if the worker wants the family group to hear a given person's point of view or feelings, he may encourage the focus on the individual and direct the rest of the family to "hear" what is being said. If, on the other hand, clearer communication is the issue, a family member may be asked to speak directly to another person and encourage this person to respond or to restate what has been said to him. (Dyadic communication).

The strategic school likes to utilize a circular way of gathering information in which a third person is asked to give his (her) opinion on the transaction or relationship of a dyad in the family. E.g., the older brother may be asked how he perceives his father's or mother's relationship with his younger sib-

ling; subsequently the younger brother may be asked
the same question regarding his older brother's relationship with a parent. Little by little pieces of
the puzzle are added to form a whole; the fact that
it is done in front of the rest of the family allows
for an experience quite different from the one a family ordinarily has.

c) DO NOT DO FOR THE FAMILY WHAT THEY CAN DO FOR
   THEMSELVES

   Since we are unable to know in advance a family's
hidden potential, it is essential to observe what a
family does in a given situation. If need be the family therapist can point to a direction and only if
this fails to work and the situation requires action
the therapist should take over. This is particularly
important in families where the parents seem to be
"helpless". If the parent can be helped to move toward assuming some responsibility this is preferable
to the worker doing something himself, even though
the worker's action may be "better suited" to the
situation than the parent's action. To give an actual example: an overwhelmed mother in a single parent
family talks to the worker while her children are engaged in increasingly frantic activity. One child
may be tugging and pulling at mother while she is
blissfully ignoring all the goings on, and may be
talking in an intense way to the worker. Finally, a
child trips and bangs her head. If the worker who
already had an increasingly uneasy feeling regarding
the mother's "non-handling" of her children now intervenes and takes the toddler on her lap and comforts
him, abruptly taking the attention away from mother,
the following is likely to occur - the child is getting the message that mother is not a ready resource,
the mother might feel either relieved by "another mother" doing for her and/or be slightly resentful that
her "child" and not the "child in her" is getting
something. On a somewhat more available level there
might be bitterness as to "how easy" it is for the ad
hoc parent to be all giving while she, the mother,
has to constantly struggle with the reality of her unruly children. This and other feelings are, of
course, just conjectures, although they have been
tested out often in similar situations to consider
them as valid. A too rapid intervention on behalf
of the child often leads the parent to despair and a
sense of helplessness, envy, or bitterness which is

often disguised and then falsely diagnosed as "dumb-
ness" (failure to learn from a model) or as resistance (unwillingness to learn). There are many ways
in which the feelings can be made real to a class but
as I have indicated the "experiential" is probably
the most potent! A "mother" can be designated from
the class-group who is told to position herself in
the middle of the class circle with 3-4 young "children" who are instructed to tug at her while she talks
to a "worker" about her unhappiness with an alcoholic
or drug-addicted husband. One of the children finally
trips and cries. Each "acting" group will "do" something different which, when discussed, will bring out
the dilemma of the worker, the feeling of the mother,
the feeling of the children. The class then can contribute alternate ways of going about dealing with
such or similar situations. In line with this one
might try to alert the class to various consequences
and have them model other possibilities, e.g., the
suggestion may be be made that the worker could prevent "escalation" by being alert to the situation
earlier, but in doing sp should try not to detour the
parent. She could, for instance, draw the attention
of the mother to the children's clamor for her attention and then encourage the mother to consider how to
deal with the situation. Whether this works or not,
discussion of "mother's need versus children's needs"
and the likelihood that ignored messages tend to escalate are issues surely germane to this kind of family. If the interaction reaches a crisis point it
is of course much harder for the worker not to take
over and indeed sometimes it is impossible. Yet, a
suggestion to the mother that now "that our conversation is interrupted" she might want to comfort
Joanie is surely preferable to the worker's taking
Joanie on her lap. If all fails, the scene can be
discussed later on or played out - learning does not
have to be done instantaneously.

Depending on the worker's presentation of the
situation in class and depending on what the instructor wants to highlight, the worker can either
be cast in the role of the observer, the mother or a
given child. Or the same person can be cast in different roles if the development of empathy is the issue.

Thus, throughout, we have dealt with the concept
of enabling and modeling, rather than "doing for",
the latter built in in the child-oriented approach

still so much part of many student-workers. While
emphasizing and showing and experiencing what may be
occurring for a particular person in the family, the
focus eventually gets back to the worker-student whose
discomfort to find himself in a difficult situation
needs to be recognized - and empathized with including
his feeling of anxiety due to temporary helplessness
when his "customary" solution to a difficult situation
(letting somebody else do rather than doing himself)
is thwarted.

There are so many possible variations on this
theme which depending on the resources of the class
(examples brought by them) and their level of experience and the phase the class is in can be further developed - like the use of sub-groups in chaotic families. In one such family which I interviewed as a
consultant before an audience, the parents however
much I encouraged their operating as rule- and deci-
sion-makers and enforcers of rules for their acting-
out, uncooperative, mostly adolescent five children,
were unable to do so. The major factor was that the
oldest son in his early twenties, recently released
from a State Hospital, was "protected" by his parents.
(One can just imagine how this may in part have been
a result of the intervention of a zealous individual
worker who may have alerted the parents to the young
man's difficulties in the re-entry to the real world).
The rest of the siblings carried a silent but potent
rebellion against this "unfairness" - which got lived
out in an almost total sit-down strike re household
chores. As the session progressed I felt an increasing sense of despair which I finally made overt saying "that I felt just as helpless as the parents".
At this point the oldest son volunteered some services and then turned to his younger siblings and engaged them in a productive discussion re their respective responsibilities which within a short time
they had divided up among themselves - much to the
surprise of the parents and last but not least of
myself.

It is not uncommon that hidden potentials in a
system come to the fore when the leader does not fill
the gap. The open expression of the therapist's helplessness became a mobilizing agent for the whole family and enabled the "weakest" member to assume leadership. This single move however should not be confused with the therapist's duplicating a helpless
role in a leaderless family. Basically the therapist-

needs to be in charge of the process, even though his move at a given point may be to call attention to his helplessness.

d) HOW TO HELP A STUDENT TO DESCRIBE A CASE

This is not as easy as it may seem since most individually programmed students will begin with detailed descriptions of either an individual background or of the diagnosis of a given person usually the target patient. I discourage this immediately by leading the student to instruct me how to draw the family on the blackboard. Thus, instead of getting a traditional case history it enables the student to show the class how a family looks schematically.

As a first step I explain that I like to draw the family as a circle which leads me to talk about family as a unit system and about the family and its boundaries.

Diagram I

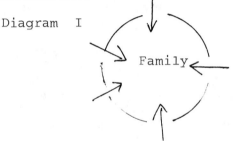

Family   Community

The boundaries cannot be fully airtight or else no "air" (new information and experience) can make its way into the family and thus no interchange between the outer system - the environment - and the family can take place; thus growth is not possible. No family can survive under these circumstances! Some families like the very isolated, the "schizophrenic", the phobic, etc. suffer to varying degrees from this syndrome. On the other hand (see diagram II) there are families whose boundaries are too loose, too much air comes in and the family has not learned to define what belongs within and what belongs without and it gets flooded by the stimuli from the outer world; thus in the extreme this family cannot survive either as family.

Diagram II

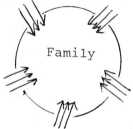

Family   Community

I question the students regarding the position and
distance of various family members. Oh blessed chalk!
Positions can be altered at will - like when parents
have first seemingly equal positions but upon further
discussion the student will indicate that father is
more of an outsider and certainly not mother's equal.
Thus what may have initially looked like this:

I.

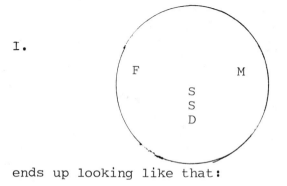

ends up looking like that:

2.

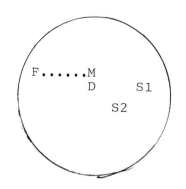

The class may then be encouraged to speculate about the "problem" in this family and they quickly will state that there is an absent father, who may appear aloof, is in a less powerful position than mother, with son #1 possibly being the parental child and son #2 the symptom carrier. Connections between the distant, often weak marital link and the emergence of the parental child are made as is some speculation regarding the outside position of the second son which may have become intensified when the youngest daughter was born displacing him from the baby position. Thus although dealing with structural phenomena we recognize the importance of time, and with it the developmental phases in the family (which is a way of looking at whether something has been going on for a long time, or not, at what phase shifts occurred, etc.)

While the family or its spokesman insists on a single focus, i.e., the discussion of THE problem, usually a symptom seen as belonging to one person, I encourage the student to watch the way the family presents itself.

After attention is paid to the family's structural characteristics, the time context in which it finds itself, speculation can begin regarding the onset of the symptom, the symptom bearer himself and the family's maintenance of the symptom. The move from a generalistic point of view to a specific stresses first the similarities existing in certain types of families; then the specific and unique aspects of the family under discussion. Students are often amazed at the accuracy of their detective work.

e) DIFFERENTIATE BETWEEN THE PROBLEM THE FAMILY PRE-
    SENTS AND WHAT SUBSEQUENTLY DEVELOPS ESPECIALLY
    IN RELATION TO THERAPEUTIC INTERVENTION

The way a family begins, the first session, reflects their basic patterns in a stress situation. Contrary to what some people perceive as the "artificiality" of the therapeutic session (or an observed session with a consultant doing the interviewing) the picture we get from the family is usually accurate though the stress accentuates and intensifies how people act. Most people will be the way they are but more so due to the anxiety experienced in a new situation - the quantity rather than the quality is different. They may be more polite, more guarded, more

28

aggressive, chatty, etc., but whatever the family's
attitude, it tells us how they deal with a stress situation, a most importamt thing to know about a family.
In some rarer cases, more often than not, young children may show themselves very different from the way
they usually are - the chatterbox may fall silent or
the relatively independent child may be clinging and
this, of course, needs to be taken into consideration
and families will usually talk about these differences.
If the behavior is due to an unaccustomed situation
it usually wears off and approximates normalcy after
a few sessions. Be it as it may actively involving
the little ones is not one of my priorities, which
differs from other family therapists who feel strongly that they want to establish quickly some relationship directly with all children in a family. In a
way I consider it as very natural that children do
not trust a stranger in a strange situation, especially in a situation where they sense their parents
are ill at ease. I usually take a wait-and-see attitude and if parents push the children to "give out"
while they are holding back, I might comment that the
children show good judgment not to trust me yet and
wonder whether the "old folks" do not share their
feelings.

I might even add that somehow children know that
chatting is not the issue and that talking about
things which are tough does take time. I quite cus-
tomarily give to my students such pointers, ice
breakers, useful tips behind which lie important
thoughts. After the students relate how a family began with them I ask them whether anything changed during the session and if so in response to what or to
whom and what the change seems to be about. I emphasize the difference between so-called spontaneous
changes, those the family manages by itself and those
which are responses to therapeutic intervention.
There are diagnostic and prognostic implications in
either change. If a student may describe quite accurately an adolescent in a family as depressed, I
usually press for more descriptive assessment such as
how she sat, looked, etc., and I question whether any
changes occurred throughout the session. "Yes, at
one point she lifted her head and smiled." "When was
this?" When her father spoke about taking her on his
lap shen she was little". "What happened then?" "The
mother interrupted, saying that this was immaterial
and that what they came here for was the girl's impossible behavior". These kinds of sequences are

often overlooked by beginners and yet what inherent
riches may be discovered once students begin to see
connections rather than content or basic characteristics. While not always clear to the presenting student, the class picks up easily that the daughter's
depression is not total, nor immovable, that she can
be touched and the person touching is her father.
They can also see that the mother does not permit the
father-daughter rapprochement to take place. Why else
would mother disturb a moment of wordless intimacy and
get back to her original harangue? At such a point an
intellectualizing student may venture to hypothesize
that father and daughter are oedipally linked; I am
unimpressed. What a message to an eager student who
wanted to display her analytical knowledge. I bring
the class back to the changing aspects - while it is
true that mother had indeed come because she was dis-
satisfied with her daughter, she had somewhere in the
session stopped to complain and resumed it only after
the interlude between father and daughter - whatever
the reason, reestablished the earlier equilibrium
through the anti-daughter stance rather than permit-
ting a father-daughter coalition. Again, dyads, coalitions, changes in the system are the focus of our
discussion rather than the psychological make-up of
the daughter-patient.

At other points in the interview things may happen which may either confirm or refute some earlier
assumption; evidence and counter-evidence serve to
broaden the picture, leading to multilevel understanding. The mother may state that daughter was so different when she was younger but that since brother
left for college she has become especially difficult.
Here again is an opportunity to talk about the important "turning points" (passages) in the life of a family, e.g., the impact of the onset of adolescence or
the actual leaving of the oldest or the youngest of
the family. Discussions often reveal profound fears
in both parents and in the young ones, though "children" may overtly display contrasting behavior.

How much learning on the basis of one brief case
example. The danger, of course, is that the class
gets dizzy when we move from topic to topic, look at
various possibilities, check them out with the "in-
formant", add new evidence, discard those which do
not seem to be valid. In order to avoid overload the
instructor needs to be aware of the group atmosphere.
Has the class reached a saturation point? Have too

many individuals gotten"lost"? Thus at this point
the group process needs to take priority over theac-
tual teaching of the subject matter.

f) THE NEED FOR A STRATEGY

    By now a lot has gotten stirred up. Some cher-
ished concepts have been questioned, things dimly
known have been touched and looked at from another
perspective not only by the instructor but by the
students themselves. Other students struggle a-
gainst "the new" - the inter-group exchange becomes
heated. The anxiety level of the class rises, partly
due to what has been shaken up, but also due to the
fact that while they now "know" how to look differently they still do not know how to help, how to intervene. Questions such as, "should we confront the family with what we see?" and, if so, "won't we lose
them?" are being asked. Examples may be given of how
this actually has already happened. All these questions reveal anxiety but they show involvement. It
means that the students are raring to go and I allow
a great deal of bombarding me with questions and general expression of feelings and thoughts. It is an
informal evaluation reflecting where we are. Misunderstandings can be cleared up more often than not,
by the students themselves; new ideas are offered,
pieces added. A few students may look lost and I may
direct myself to them. If I miss the non-verbal plea
of those less ready to articulate their doubts, they
may flounder and in extreme cases remain confused,
something I may only detect at the time of the written
assignment - the last and in a way most important connection (transaction) between myself, the instructor,
and my students. But I am moving too far ahead. Suf-
fice it to say that however rich the content, however
much the class seems engaged, time must be taken to
catch one's breath, to insure maximum contact with
the whole group and to help with the process of integration.
    Once this is done I deal with the actual content
of when and how to transmit to the family the therapist's observations and impressions. (Comments and
questions seem preferable to interpretation). This
is a good place to speak about differences among practitioners. Some separate the study phase from the
treatment phase. Decisions are made in staff confer-
ences where various experts on the basis of their observations (interviews with sub-groups or tests ad-

ministered) will together with the family therapist fit the puzzle together and the recommendations are transmitted to the family whose part in the process is piecemal and often fragmented.

I, however, together with the majority of family therapists, believe in rapid if not immediate engagement of the family on the basis of their playing out their drama or comedy as the case may be. My own inclination which I identify to the students, and in more advanced classes may juxtapose to alternate ways of doing things, stems from the belief that only through engagement the family gets to "know" what family treatment is all about and can make a commitment to it. I do not believe that a mere explanation that we work with family units is sufficient although in the initial negotiation with the family the conviction of the therapist as well as his use of authority do play an important part which aids the family to make a commitment.

In the initial family session the student is encouraged to begin less by responding to whatever the family's presenting problem is, but by referring to the actual situation, namely to the fact that the family is gathered together in a strange place facing a stranger for the purpose of getting some help. While encouraging some response to this the therapist needs to pay attention to the unique way in which a family introduces itself through the roles they carry, the behavior patterns they display and the emotional quality of their communication. This is not easy for the beginner who himself has to cope with his anxiety and it is likely that he may fall back to history-taking or letting the family engage in complaints. Instead I suggest that the student therapist comments on some phenomena which he has noticed thus far e.g., that "in your family the women seem to be the talkers", or somewhat later yet "I notice that when I ask your wife a question you answer for her". There will be responses to these comments, defensive ones, clarifying ones, others adding new information, all of which leading to a mutual engagement and alerting the family to what the therapist pays attention to. Some self-consciousness is unavoidable, yet sometimes surprising changes in behavior can be noticed which alert the therapist to touchy areas as well as those which can easily be changed. Even defensive statements like a woman's "oh I only do this here" when accompanied by a lifted eyebrow of one or a giggle on

the part of another family member gives valuable
hints to the therapist regarding feelings, attitudes
and family trans-actions. Even in a first session a
child can be encouraged to "say with his mouth" what
he has said with a gesture. Thus new possibilities
are being introduced such as that people can directly
talk to each other rather than that they talk about
each other and that there are many ways in which a
person can express himself.

This approach does indeed acculturate a family to
a new maybe a bit frightening but also intriguing way
of operating. Comments like the one cited above are
often called"confrontations' or "interpretations" but
they are really nothing else but selected articulat-
ions of observations which have to do with interpersonal behavior or clarification of non-verbal messages such as seating arrangements, body postures and
gestures. They are tentatively made statements geared
to make the family aware of areas in their life they
either may not be aware of or may consider as unimportant or not connected to what they are here for.
The family's response to these comments brings about
a level of engagement different from what is traditionally occurring in a first session. There is thus
a constant sharing and testing, a moving forward and
backward that characterizes the initial engagement
which at the end of the session needs to lead to some
tentative observations about the family as a whole and
some linkage to the "problem" as well as the direction
therapist and family will need to follow. It is based
on the therapist's perception of the family, their reaction to the process and, of course, to exploration
of the content which includes some idea as to what
created the current family imbalance. It is thus
not sufficient to just state to the family that they
need to return the following week but some albeit
very tentative commitment needs to be negotiated which,
of course, depends on the family's reaction to the
session itself. If the session was worth its salt it
surely must have aroused all kinds of feelings which
to the extent that they are expressed lose some of
the power to become acted out after the session. This
is especially important for family members who were
reluctant to start or for those for whom too little or
too much occurred in the session. Many beginners have
found themselves either elated or in despair after a
session but never checked out the family's reaction.
If they would have done so a bridge could have been
built to the next session. Some beginning family

33

therapists become so interested in family transactions that they neglect to get pertinent information about what brings the family into treatment, the character of the difficulty and how the family has been dealing with it. In all initial interviews an assessment has to be made to discern whether a family is in immediate danger or whether the difficulties are chronic.

Different family therapists will go about gathering information in different ways - some of them can be combined, others not. A structural family therapist approaches a family through instant engagement in the presence, tracking family sequences, checking on roles and positions and then proceeds in the session itself to change boundaries and shift inter-generational lines.

The strategically oriented family therapist[1], as stated earlier, will collect data by taking a neutral position, asking the opinion of one person in relation to others until such point when he is ready to formulate a hypothesis on which subsequent moves are based.

Followers of Bowen tend to advocate staying out of the emotionally charged family field, and work with the most available and motivated sub-system (sometimes one single person). Through coaching he aims to influence the rest of the system, a method which is also productively used in the training of students.

Haley, Whitacker, Satir and the psychodynamic school of family therapists, all have their own way of beginnings, collecting information, and techniques with which they hope to achieve change in the family. The student is encouraged to read, and some of the differences in the approach are being discussed in class. However, my basic aim as a teacher is to familiarize the student with a way of observing, thinking and ordering data which will enable him to work with a family in systemic terms.

Throughout the life of the class issues and questions are being taken up repeatedly since teaching like treating is an endless repetition of basic points which constantly need to be sharpened and dealt with in a different context until they become part of the student's body of knowledge and his professional Self. Hence very early in the semester I will refer to a

34

family's structure or organization or a family's specific developmental state or to the emotional character of a family. Phenomena related to them are pointed out, like the emergence of the parental child in a single parent family, the relationship between the weak marital axis and the inter-generational coalition, the importance of the sibling sub-system, power issues, communication, etc. are identified in examples as they are presented. They lead to a discussion of possible interventive direction which may lead to immediate or more far reaching goals.

CHAPTER IV

FAMILY TYPOLOGY

Early in the semester, whether done in orderly sequences or in bits and pieces, depending on what is
occurring in the classroom, the students are introduced to the classification of family types. Some of
these classification are well-known in the literature,
though called by different names, and some have been
labeled by me. Any attempt to classify defines families in gross terms: like a caricature. Subtle-
ties and movement, however, come to life through the
transactions and the feelings, expressed through
words and behavior. Classification facilitates a basic way of looking, grasping and describing a family;
it provides a family blueprint. (The Germans call it
a Bauplan), which may lead to a reconstruction of components which do not fit.

The family, like all other systems has its own
organization which characterizes and affects the
life patterns of its parts. The way a family is organized can be viewed in three major ways: (I) structurally, (II) developmentally, and (III) through assessing the major psychological characteristics of
the family. (Family climate).

I. FAMILY STRUCTURE

A family structure* can be viewed (much the same
as a building) from its basic framework or as the
body is viewed from its skeleton. It determines, in

_____

*Dr. Salvador Minuchin uses "structural intervention"
as a treatment approach which is aimed to reorganize
some structural components of a family to enable it
to function more adequately e.g., delineation of the
inter-generational sub-systems, changing of coali-

37

a most basic way, the functioning of the system.
Through it the family is being held together and it
cannot be totally changed lest the family disin-
tegrates. However, the component parts of the structure can be rearranged. To be more specific: that a
family consists of one parent and three children IS a
structural phenomenon which determines certain family
positions and coalitions and profoundly influences the
system. Changes can occur through altering positions
and coalitions, through the realignment of sub-groups
which may create new alliances, which in turn influence people's feelings, thoughts, attitudes and
actions.

It always startles me to observe how loaded and
emotionally charged any discussion of structure is.
The most common questions have to do with those challenging my value judgment - the fact that I usually
begin with the "intact" family seems to imply for
many students that what is not "intact" is somehow
"less good or less desirable". Other questions have
to do with a currently touchy issue namely why a
couple which decides not to have children is not considered a family, or whether a family with adopted
children is an "intact" one. It requires a great deal
of reassurance to convince the group that a structure
is neither good nor bad, although most families consist of a parental pair whose task is to procreate
and raise young ones. There are, of course, many
variations depending on cultural traditions, societal
needs and on fate (e.g., death) which change the basic structure and lead to a shrinking or expanding of
families. Family therapy or family intervention is
applicable to all families whatever their structural
uniqueness. It is, in fact, extremely helpful for

---

*(ctd. from preceding page)

tions, distancing of sub-groups, etc. In the book,
Families and Family Therapy by Salvador Minuchin,
Harvard University Press, Cambridge, Mass. 1974
(Chapter 3, p. 51) he states: "Family structure is
the invisible set of functional demands that organizes the ways in which family members interact. A
family is a system that operates through transactional patterns ... they are maintained by two systems
of constraint, the first generic, and the second
idiosyncratic, involving the mutual expectations of
particular family members".

young couples without children, especially those
where partners may be closely tied to their families
of origin. This means that the major significant
transactions (whether played out through over-involvement or extreme distancing) are geared as much to the
family of origin as they are to the marital partner.
Many family therapists including myself like to involve the families of origin in treatment, though not
necessarily on a regular basis.

The Intact Family

The intact family is a bio-social unit which consists of two generations living together. They are a
parental pair (married or not) and their offspring.
The organization of the family is affected by such
factors as the number of children and their spacing,
the gender distribution, the ages of the parents,
racial composition and the like.

Schematically it looks this way:

As can be seen each spouse carries a double role: the
role of the married partner and of the parent. If one
role becomes so dominant that the other role recedes
and if this occurs over a long period of time, dysfunctional patterns become established. The natural
division in any family occurs along generational lines.
Parents are ALWAYS older than their children. This
fact of nature determines the most important function
of the parental role: caretaker, protector, socializ-
er and educator of the young ones. If the generational boundary line is blurred the children either become adults prematurely or the adults function as children. However, this reversal of roles can never be
total or else the family could not exist, but too

great fluctuation between roles creates confusion and instability which tends to lead to a dysfunctioning system.

The discussion then turns to families with other structures: the Single Parent Family, the Intergenerational Family, the Reconstituted (by some now called the "blended family"), and other family variations. Since the basic structure determines organization of the unit, there are consequences which emanate from a certain structure creating certain phenomena (syndromes) like "The Parental Child" in the single parent family, "Split Loyalties" and "Alliances" on the part of children when parents are separated (remarried or not), the my, your, and our child syndrome in the reconstituted family. While these are recurrent features typical for a certain structure they can also appear in other families under certain circumstances. The meaning and intensity of the phenomena and the intervention which is needed will be different depending on whether it is predominantly a structural - situational phenomenon or one which stems from interpersonal disturbances. To be more specific: split loyalty can occur in intact families where both parents are feuding, although if the children are not pulled into the marital fight, they can remain relatively unscathed. In fact the most effective therapeutic intervention is greared to extricating the children from the marital fight. However, when the marital split has already occurred, a child cannot help but feel pulled into the direction of the missing parent whether the pull or the loyalty is lived out as wishing to live with the absent parent or as not wanting to have anything to do with the "deserter". This in part depends on previous family messages.

As a teaching tool the graphic representation or the playing out of the situation through structured role playing is helpful.

The Single Parent (SP) Family[1]

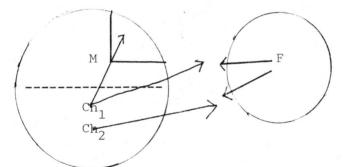

The SP* family is either a transitory or permanent family arrangement. There are two types of SP families;
the one which starts as a SP family (the OOW mother
and her children) and the other which starts as an intact family, but due to circumstances loses a parent.
The two predominant reasons for this loss are death
and divorce. In both these instances a new adaptation
is necessary since the gap which is left by the missing parent needs to be filled. The one who is most
likely to fill it is either the oldest (oldest remaining) or the child of the opposite sex from the remaining parent, depending on other factors in the family.
This leads to the emergence of the "parental child".
Realistic factors play a part in this propelling move,
which leads to a change in the sibling sub-system and
brings about an inter-generational coalition with occasional unfortunate consequences. The child has to
become prematurely an adult (pseudo-adult), the siblings envy his position of power and thus the parental
child is both favored and overburdened. Yet what can
a parent who is left as lone adult do but "feel" lonely and overwhelmed by too many added demands on the
part of their now needier children whose life too has
changed. In the process one child may be "chosen" to
follow the parent's implicit demands for a pseudo-
partner. Thus the emergence of the parental child is
not necessarily due to the "infantile" nature of a
mother or her "weak ego" though she may or may not
suffer from these "impairments". Whatever they are,
they become intensified by the change of structure.

---

*To call the family in which a marital partner is di-
vorced or separated a Single Parent family is a mis-
nomer since, indeed, there are two parents living!

The difference between a SP family where one parent had died and one where a parent lives elsewhere has to do with one being a self-sustaining system and the other one being an inter-dependent one. The kind of relationship the two units have with one another depend on the ability of the two adults - the parents - to divest themselves of their marital role while maintaining their parental role, albeit in a modified way. Parenthood after all is a non-divorceable item!

For many students to look upon a situation in this way is an eye-opener since they have been accustomed to looking at individuals and families primarily in pathological terms. There are other students who have been programmed to minimize the existence of emotional difficulties and see most phenomena as the result of faulty social situations and processes (poverty, discrimination, etc.). These are certainly important factors as are a person's or a family's emotional vulnerability, but given both the external and the internal factors, the family structure may either aid or hinder the way a family can deal with these stresses. Hence structure is emphasized as an important variable which removes judgmental attitudes on the part of the therapist and decreases guilt, blame and shame on the part of the family.

To make this point more vivid the students are encouraged to "imagine" what would happen to them as people and as families if - to give an example - a parental child in a Single Parent family reaches adolescence and begins to "neglect" the place in his family she or he so far has carried for the mutual benefit of all. The fact that Joanie, 16, has acquired a boyfriend and no longer shares with mother the tasks of rearing the younger siblings, to be her confidante and companion, may well throw the family out of kilter. Naturally, the mother finds fault with the boyfriend. The girl on the other hand, in her attempt to satisfy the multiple demands of the "self", the family and the school, may develop a school phobia; three tasks are too many, so one has to be dropped. The family is rarely aware of what brought about the turbulence. Complaints or symptoms are the SOS signals, but often not understood by the student-worker. Whatever the interventive device decided upon, the student-worker needs to grasp what the situation is about which includes a sense of what is happening to the family rather than being swayed by "over-identification" with mother, daughter,

42

or the siblings. Interventive devices may range
from heightening the family awareness to giving the
family tasks or to formulate a strategy which is aimed at bringing about a better balance. Some family
therapists use a combined approach.

The Reconstituted Family

In the reconstituted family we see how various
systems influence each other

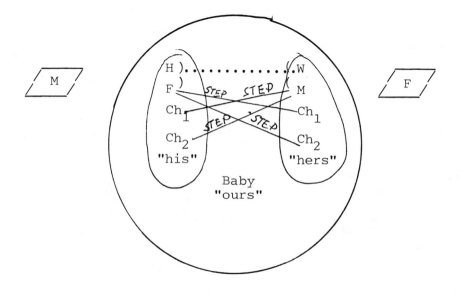

There are, of course, any number of variations in
this kind of family. The one shown in the diagram is
the most complex one in which both spouses have children not only from an earlier union, but both have
their children living with them in the same household
while at the same time a child is born to both of them.
The "his" "hers" and "ours" refer to the three sub-
groups comprising this family in which only one sub-
group shares both parents. Each parent forms a natural alliance with his/her children, an alliance which
is based on blood, heredity and a shared history. The
reconstituted family in fact is the only family struc-

43

ture which is governed by a different <u>time</u> <u>sequence</u>, namely one in which the parental unit precedes the marital unit. Thus the parent-child unit shares a joint past which experienced loss and trauma and had to pass various transitions; one of them most likely a SP stage. Because the marital relationship follows the parent-child one it tends to be weak and the marital adaptation gets often confused with the parental which means that the children get easily triangulated.

In dealing with these families two other issues are of importance. One has to do with the amount of time the newly blended family has been together and how well the tasks of the prior stages have been fulfilled; the other has to do with turf. Which family group had to move and which family stayed in their accustomed territory. Many conflicts in this type of family are related to unresolved and often unexpressed feelings regarding these matters.

In the majority of reconstituted families, however, the new spouse is added to a natural unit headed by a single parent. If the step-parent has no children of his own, he is a newcomer to the world of children. In any event the step-parent is and to an extent always will be an outsider due to the fact that she/he has not shared the family group's life history. This "Johnny come lately" syndrome is a natural consequence of the structure which often leads to feelings of over-sensitivity and over-expectation, followed by disappointment in oneself and others. This fact is further complicated by a variety of myths[2] regarding the character of step-parents, myths which have been transmitted from generations to generations and are deeply embedded in our culture. Each family member in the new unit has to struggle. The caretaker parent is busy to establish a new relationahip yet feels torn between his allegiance to her/his children and the need for and obligations to a new spouse. He often bemoans the lack of interest of this person in her/his children, yet fails to delegate responsibility for daily child rearing to the step-parent.

The step-parent in turn tends to feel like the eternal outsider who never "quite makes it" with the stepchildren whether he deals with his feelings by staying aloof or becoming a "seducer".

The parent who has left often envies and therefore criticizes both his former spouse and the step-
parent whether the underlying motive is guilt or a
profound sense of loss.[3]

Needless to say that the children, products of an
earlier marriage which ended in a breakup, are torn
by their own feelings and by the existing pulls transmitted through both overt and subtle messages. They
are haunted by split loyalties which make commitment
to the new family unit difficult. This is not a phantasy but is due to the reality of one parent being
the "holiday" parent, more concerned with giving the
children a good time and with keeping or regaining
their love, than to helping the former spouse with
disciplinary issues or with making difficult decisions
affecting the children. In a way the child's position
is somewhat paradoxical: the more he begins to like
the step-parent, the more he may feel disloyal to his
natural parent. Allowing sufficient time for gradual
resolution is essential.

Stereotypes and unrealistic expectations abound
in these units and make a complex situation unneces-
sarily difficult. The myth of the "wicked stepmother"
and the hope for the "instant love or magic cure" for
whatever ails the family are recurrent phenomena which
appear in many of these families. All this, the
structure, the situation and the feelings and attitudes stemming from them put a heavy burden on the system. Yet, inherent in these newly formed units are
new potentials which can lead to better regrouping
and growth. Thus each family unit has a profound impact on the other, and the family therapist has a
unique chance to enable the various units to come together and negotiate a new balance.

Once the scheme is designed or played out, students are able to identify many of the above described situations and feelings including the dilemma
in which each unit finds itself. Of course, much
personal material tends to come out. Yet, as connections are made, most students begin to see the
issues rather than viewing things only through the
eyes of one individual, be it the torn child or the
angry mother. They begin to see the field as an
arena in which transactions are being enacted, determined by the structure as much as by the individual makeup of the people.

Talking about structure is not a dull matter but
one which stimulates a lot of feelings since every
student comes from one or the other family type and
has participated in and/or suffered from alliances,
coalitions, family positions and the like. Often
students will timidly share with me that I have just
described his family to the class to a "T". I suspect that this occurs more often in classes on family
therapy than in classes where individual growth and
development are discussed, largely because of the
emphasis on the experiential. Similarly, actual family tratment sessions tend to stir up more emotions
than sessions with an individual since the total situation which often creates pain, or discomfort is
brought right into the treatment situation. I am
somewhat puzzled by the fact that often after "discussions" about structure, the class expresses some
despair. It is as if the fact that there is a certain structure is seen by the students as immutable.
This strikes me as curious since many mental health
professionals are taught that part of their task as
a helper is to become a temporary substitute parent
especially to those who have been sorely deprived.
Not only does this reinforce omnipotence; it is, in
my opinion, a misunderstood concept. Firstly because
what lacks lies usually in a person's past (childhood deprivation or trauma) for which there is simply
no making up, and secondly, because it is naive to
believe that even the most meaningful, once-a-week
relationship could fill the void. Thus worker and
client alike are burdened by an unreal expectation:
somehow life will make up for early hurts or that
the step-parent can fill not only the vacant space
but make up for what the natural parent has failed
to do. The family therapist, in contrast, works towards utilizing the family's dormant potential. Instead of mothering a needy person, he seeks to help
the family members find ways to nurture each other.

Whatever the reason for the despair, the class
needs to be allowed to live through the momentary
hopelessness. Once this has taken place we can get
back to the difference between the overt recognition
of "what is", what a situation tends to arouse in family members - and in which direction the family can
move to mitigate their pain. This does not occur by
making a family into another kind of family but by
helping them to recognize how the situation is affecting them. The family needs to be helped to be in
touch with their unrealistic expectations, their

guilt, their shame, their anger, and most importantly, with their inherent strength. The techniques to achieve this may vary, depending on which family therapy approach one subscribes to. Most important, however, is the message conveyed to the family by the family therapist: it is not a question of blame, but largely the result of a combination of human interactions which may be unravelled.

It is often not clear to families that their so-called "non-problem-child" is also affected by the family structure and the issues related to it. In fact such a child may, at times,envy the scapegoated child for the attention he gets. The "our" child in a femily, the one born to both parents in a reconstituted family who is seen by everybody as the privileged one, may envy his half siblings' weekly visits to his natural parent. What a revelation if these usually unspoken thoughts are brought out into the open! What a boost for the "bad" (step) child who perceived himself as being in the most unfavorable position in the family! The next step is to help the family find a way to deal with the situation differently; to decrease the dysfunctioning, whether it is expressed in threats of expulsion or marital discord.

The Intergenerational Family

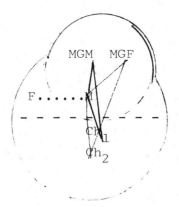

----

*MGM = Maternal Grandmother
 MGF = Maternal Grandfather

47

This type of family has been the prototype of family structure in the past and is still quite prevalent in some cultures. In the intergenerational family, three generations live together in the same house. In our culture where young adults are expected to live independently from their elders, this fact alone may indicate some malfunctioning. However, in many subcultures the three-generational living arrangement is seen as natural and does not necessarily connote any problem with separation. For instance among the black poor, adolescent and young adult children especially when they are unmarried continue to live with their parents (sometimes families headed by women only) or they rejoin the household of their parents when they have children and are not able to sustain themselves as a separate unit. Many of these households are matriarchal - headed by the older woman who takes care of her grandchildren and often greatnieces and -nephews.

The outstanding phenomenon in these types of families is related to the inherent lack of clarity regarding roles and authority, e.g., who for instance is the head of the household and who is in charge of whom. The unclarity is in part rooted in the fact that the parent of the child is at the same time the child of the parent (grandmother). Not that the roles need to be confused, but they have to be constantly switched or have to operate simultaneously, something which often creates confusion. A child in such a family often does not know in whom the authority is invested since while a parent may make one rule, a grandparent may circumvent it or carry an attitude that they not their adult children know what's best for the little ones. In view of the fact that these things tend to get transacted rather than discussed, the chances of subtle maneuvering, collusion and coalitions are greater than in other types of families. Hence, like the child who is put in a position to manipulate between the feuding parents, in this kind of family, the manipulation takes place between parent and grandparent. Triangulation, which is so often a sign of malfunctioning in two-generational households, gets multiplied here since all transactions tend to be more complex and more covert (they involve more people and an additional generation). The husbands (fathers)in these kinds of households feel often without power against what seems to them an awesome unit consisting of daughter and her parents with the women often more closely tied. Whatever the position of the

young husband, he can hardly win if he sides with
his wife against her critical mother, the same wife
chides him for doing so and if he withdraws he will
be called an uninterested husband and thus give further justification to the mother-daughter coalition.
There is no winner in these situations since both
grandparents and parents are deprived of their legit-
imate role and power. Interestingly, coalitions in
these families are not necessarily drawn by lines of
blood and thus differ from the reconstituted family.

In a family which I recently interviewed in front
of the class, we learned that the son-in-law whenever
he had a fuss with his wife went to his mother-in-law
to complain. This made the old lady very proud because of the aura of impartiality this gave to her.
The price paid for this, however, was the daughter's
bitterness due to her feeling of being deserted by
both mother and husband. This fanned the marital
conflict since the wife could express anger against
her husband but not against her mother.

I do not want to give the impression that all intergenerational families have to have these kinds of
problems, just that the likelihood of interference
and enmeshment, role reversal and confusion are greater in this structure. On the other hand, this family
has ready-made support systems for all three generations which otherwise are not easily available in our
urban family culture. Even the lack of privacy existing in these families can be made up by the couple's
greater freedom to go out together because there are
grandparents who are the natural babysitters. Or the
tired working mother may be helped by a grandmother
in the home who is willing to take over some duties.
The proximity which breeds intrusion may also produce
intimacy between generations which would otherwise be
missing. Both the intergenerational as well as the
reconstituted family have dimensions available which
when not misused and channeled in the proper direction can add to the riches of family living.

II. DEVELOPMENTAL STAGES

Yet another way to view a family is through its
developmental stages. This classification is an adaptation from Erickson who called attention to the
importance of the developmental stages of individuals.[4] It has equal importance for families. Family

assessment and intervention will in large measure depend on the developmental phase the family is in. Family therapy literature refers to developmental phases[6] of families as "family turning points"[5]. Families[6] move from one stage to another requiring different adaptations for the whole unit, not just for the individuals who also are experiencing changes in developmental states (like the oldest child who enters adolescence). Thus, a family which may have been able to live through and negotiate an earlier stage in which nurturing and protection was the primary task may, at the point of adolescence, suddenly find itself in trouble! Some subtle danger signals may have existed at an earlier stage, but as long as the family managed without great distress neither the family nor society considers it to be a problem. It may sound somewhat absurd for those of us who are accustomed to view difficulties in individual terms when I talk about an "adolescent family", yet from my point of reference as soon as the oldest child becomes an adolescent the family is in a crisis state. It is a period in which the total unit is in a temporary state of upheaval since significant shifts are taking place which require special adaptation on the part of all family members.

Whether or not the family succeeds in managing this or any other stage depends on the make-up of the family (its structure) and its morphostatic and morphogenetic qualities. A family needs both stability to survive various "shock experiences" and at the same time flexibility to deal with change (growth and differences). Another important issue especially germane to a "family's adolescence" has to do with the influence of the outer system which becomes increasingly important for the young person who ventures into the world at large. If the outer system is perceived by the family as too different and, therefore, potentially too threatening, the family in an effort to protect itself, may become more rigid at the very moment when its boundaries need to be flexible and open. This occurred during periods of rapid upheavals of the hectic 'sixties. It is also apparent when families migrate from one culture to another. Under such circumstances the adolescent whose task it is to find a way into the outer world through separation from the family's fold while still being supported by it (in both tangible as well as intangible ways - like getting approval for moving away or at least not being held back) will have a difficult time,

50

as will his family. The degree to which a family
manages this stage has profound repercussions for
the younger children who may misread their family's
turbulence as "if one gets older the parents do not
love one". This, in turn, may be a factor in the
younger child's determination not to grow up.

It is important to differentiate between the "developmental"and the "outer" crisis. Whereas, all
families have to live through the developmental
stages, only certain families suffer from "outer"
crises like the crisis of premature death, serious
and protracted illness, unemployment, emigration and
many other possible crises. In fact it is often an
outer event which creates a considerable imbalance in
a family. If a family finds itself taxed by demands
due to a new developmental stage, even an event which
may under ordinary circumstances have been manageable,
may now throw the family into a crisis. An example
would be a family's moving to a new neighborhood just
at the time of early adolescence of one of its children, a period when peer relationships are of great
importance. The youngster having lost his old friends,
may now find himself isolated and withdraw or may be
all too eager to form new relationships and get into
"bad" company. A ripple effect may set in which affects the whole family - coloring the parents' attitude to the child and vice versa. While individually
oriented therapists tend to see these events as affecting a given individual on whom treatment gets
focused, family therapists see any event (outer and
inner) as having impact on the whole system. The
death of a maternal grandmother may set off a depression in the mother, but the family therapist unlike
the individual therapist will address himself to this
as a family event and not just an intrapsychic disturbance. He will be attuned to how a family deals
with the mother-wife's depression and what consequences the event had on the whole family. His intervention may be geared to enable the family to be
less allergic to mother's moods, or by enabling the
subsystems to take over mother's job, temporarily.
He will keep in mind how this affects the mother. If
children suddenly do more for themselves, mother may
feel "unneeded-unemployed" and become more depressed.
Interventions need to be considered in systems'terms.

III. FAMILY CLIMATE

A third say of classifying a family or describing

51

family types is based on the psychodynamic description of family characteristics which create family patterns and become entrenched. Without claiming to be complete in my categorization and indebted to other family therapists who may or may not have given them the same names (labels) and emphasizing to the students that few families come in "pure" form. The classification in my view consists of: "the autocratic rigidified family", "the chaotic, acting-out family", "the enmeshed family", and the "depressed isolated family".

The Autocratic Rigidified Family[*]

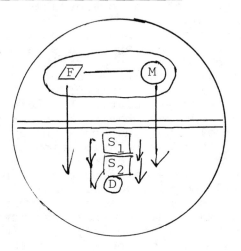

This family has clear boundaries which separate and differentiate the parents from the children and each child from each other. The line between the generations is firmly drawn, as are the boundaries between the family and the outside world. This type of family is hierarchically oriented and power and status is invested according to age and gender. Aggression is directed towards the less powerful one, who in turn directs it to the next in line with the possible exception of the youngest who even in these families may remain the pampered baby - the receiver of affection.

---

[*]In describing this family I call attention to the fact that the labels chosen by me carry some negative connotations and that it is the very extremity which makes for difficulties but that for learning purposes this is permissible.

The class is asked to formulate both the strength and likely weaknesses of this system and to guess at which developmental phases it may encounter the greatest difficulty. While I occasionally "relabel" some statements by a student, add and clarify a point here and there, the class is in general able to identify that this kind of family is _clear_ in its role structure, respective positions, and communications which include rules and consequences for violating them. Thus, in these families, there is a great deal of predictability of behavior and order which, in the eyes of young children means "security". Moreover, the boundaries between the generations are clear - there is no mistaken notion who the parents and who the children are - gender and age differences are hierarchically determined and honored. Communications are of the "the older knows best" variety and are heavily tinged with "right" or "wrong" adjectives.

This kind of family is tradition bound and there are many culturally transmitted customs which allow for a certain variety of behavior. The woman is permitted to be more emotional, the father more rational and in charge of discipline. Children in these families are exposed to two necessary ingredients essential for their growth: love and rules (discipline). The parents are a clearly defined complementary unit. In these families there is little question regarding the rights and privileges of the oldest, the boy, the girl.

What then are some of the pathological consequences which may come from this kind of structure? What might be the typical symptom in such a family and when is it most likely to occur, given other life contingencies and depending on the extremity of the behavior which often occurs in a rigid system? Due to the fact that aggression is not allowed to be expressed against the stronger, the more powerful one, there is a natural tendency in these systems to "pass the buck", e.g., give it to the weaker one or to "scapegoat" e.g., blame the most vulnerable one. Thus the movement is downward when it comes to living out obedience. (In the larger society many institutions and even some nations are modeled in this way).

<pre>
  ⌈ passing the buck
  │
  ↓ ⌈ obedience to authority
    │
</pre>

The youngest, the baby, is often excluded from this pattern so that, in some instances it is the next to the youngest child who gets it without being able to "give it" to somebody else. What a plight for this child who obeying the family rule "to give it to the one in less power" has no way to go - hence his aggression might be directed to the "stand in" siblings - other peers, or it may become internalized. Needless to say, unless we as therapists understand this "rule" and make it overt, we cannot expect the family which considers it normal to alter it.

Sibling Fighting may be rampant because of the reasons discussed above especially if the younger ones move up in the power scale. Tattletaling or spying may be rewarded and, in time, becomes institutionalized and helps shape character. Expectations are high and clearly spelled out and especially invested in the first-born. Due to the inherent rigidity of the system trouble often occurs during developmental transition points especially in adolescence. This is the period when the young ones prompted by their developmental necessities begin to branch out, "adopt" other authorities and peers as opinion shapers, and fight existing family rules. This tends to occur mostly when due to rapid changes the societal culture is in flux and moves against the family's mores, or when there is a move from one society to another (rural to urban, country to other country). Because this family type has allergies against differences even small infractions are seen and punished as major "sins". Consequently the children often resort to extreme measures to gain their freedom, running away or being especially "bad". They flaunt with glee what is most holy to the family. The family defends itself against this by scapegoating the one who is too different. Lest the system gets too much off course, the other children need to make up by being doubly good. This leads to polarization among the siblings. I emphasize that some of the same behavior (like scapegoating) occurs in other family types, but the reasons and the context in which it occurs are different. Therefore, different intervention is required. For instance, scapegoating can occur in a family where there are no rules and the parents are in weak positions, but upon closer look scapegoating may be targeted on many children in the family rather than one. It may stem from parental helplessness and the lack of rules and predictability. At this point the class may discuss how to change the system. The direction in which movement has to occur becomes clear once the assessment has been made and what the system either lacks or in what areas it is overdeveloped becomes defined. In the autocratic family, the boundary lines between the generations are too rigid and they have to be loosened so that richer and wider communication can occur. Role changing strategy is especially effective here since it enables members to "feel" what the other person feels or to begin to see the world in a different light. Changing of customary positions may enable a family to appreciate what it feels to be "small and helpless". For example, in the treatment process, a parent may be encouraged to give up the prestigious chair or is asked to sit on the floor. It is hard to be autocratic from that position, and memories of one's own powerless childhood may emerge. Thus a change in seating arrangements may help to lower defenses, bring out memories, and enable children to see their parents in a different light while at the same time the parents are being blocked from behaving in their accustomed ways. This type of exercise is also useful to students. Their feelings too get stirred up when positions are changed.

The Chaotic, Acting-out Family

(Often called impulse-ridden or infantile)

Characteristics are weak boundaries toward the outside world - little distinction between parents and children in terms of position; roles are easily interchanged and the system and its members are in perpetual motion. The marital-parental axis is weak; one would need a movie camera to capture it.

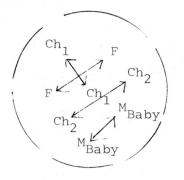

This type of family exists often among very young people, like teenage couples, drug abusers, and runaway adolescents. Their own lack of planfulness makes family planning unlikely and they tend to have children in rapid succession. Because the marital axis is very weak, splits occur frequently and may lead to the Single Parent Families, usually a young mother and several children. In this family the parent's position shifts easily, is not well-defined and lacks power. Coalitions are ever-changing and rules, to the extent that they exist, are often contradictory and tend to reflect powerlessness, or rules may be expressions of a momentary mood rather than a response to a situation. The students easily recognize that there cannot be order in such a family, hence little predictability exists leading to increased general insecurity and a constant anxiety. Erratic behavior, testing and manipulating on the part of the children and, in extreme cases, violence, often in the form of child abuse may characterize the "chaotic" family. Parents feel chronically overwhelmed; they tend to act first and think later and almost always are driven by emotions and impulses. The children have poor role models. In an effort to cope these families develop functioning sub-systems using the children who act in loco parentis. This may lead to considerable exploitation. Yet the development of a strong sub-system can be a very stabilizing factor for these families especially if the siblings are being supported by outer systems like grandparents or institutional facilities.

Another characteristic which is related to the syndrome of the overwhelmed parent is the lack of individualization which exists. This leads often to the random punishment of all children or of the child who is most available. Punishment is indiscriminate and not the consequence of a certain act or directed against a certain person (e.g., in a family where one child is being scapegoated because he is he). It is not uncommon that these parents turn to a social agency and ask for placement "of all of them". Parents like this do tend to totalize and to look for drastic solutions like placement or desertion. They rarely follow through or sustain their impulsive threats. The threats become "tools of impotence".

Students readily see that the number one priority for this kind of family is the establishment of

order; otherwise nothing else can be accomplished.
Thus, in the leaderless family, the therapist has to
assume temporary leadership or else he too will become helpless. The therapist will need to mobilize
the inherent potential of the family so that eventually its members can assume the kind of leadership
which will enhance their functioning. In the process,
the therapist will do everything he can to strengthen
the parental roles, work with the parental child or
children and will be a model to the family by helping
them to make basic rules and focus on priorities.
Students often laugh when I role-play the "rigid"
therapist: I will establish my authority and be
clearly in command, will insist that parents be listened to and that children talk according to their
ages - "the oldest first". I may structure tasks and
insist on organized discussion. This is, of course,
in contrast to the way the therapist needs to be with
rigid families. There he may need to become vague, a
bit sloppy and allow or even encourage cross-discus-
sion. He may even insist that the family listen to
the youngest because he may just express something
very meaningful, thus giving weight to the weakest.
This therapeutic move may appear to be in contradiction to Minuchin's technique of joining the family,
since it contains elements of modeling another behavior while it joins with the hidden family potential. The family therapist, however, has to be ever
sensitive to what the system can tolerate at a given
point lest the family feels it as a put-down.

The Enmeshed Family

("We" syndrome; pseudo-mutuality)

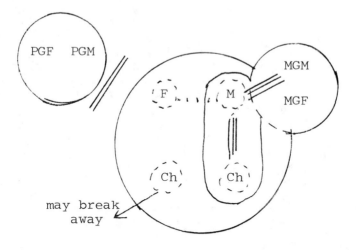

The enmeshed family is a family where the inter-
generational boundaries between the nuclear family
and the family of origin are blurred and where the
major emotionally meaningful transactions take place
between at least one spouse and his (her) parents and
other related kin. As a consequence, as can be seen
on the diagram, the marital axis is weak while at the
same time one child may be singled out to be the target of a symbiotic relationship. In general this
type of family tends to operate as a relatively closed
system. It maintains airtight boundaries against the
outside world which is experienced as dangerous. All
sub-groups have unclear boundaries vis-à-vis each
other, but some like a mother and a child are especially enmeshed. In these families the children
who are least enmeshed may be saved through benign

---

* MGM = maternal grandmother
  MGF = maternal grandfather
  PGF = paternal grandfather
  PGM = paternal grandmother

neglect. There are multiple reasons why one child is selected to become symbiotic with the mother; his position in the family, his gender, his looks may make him more vulnerable. Mother-child symbiosis is more frequent than father-child symbiosis. The latter sometimes occurs in some families where the mother is missing. Enmeshed families can be relatively easily recognized by the outside observer, although their transactions are not as obvious as those of a chaotic family. Their bonds are often subtly woven. And the denial of the existence of the enmeshment and other syndromes is typical because these families operate on "what is is not". Certain facts about relationships tend to be visible expressions of feelings denied and invalidated. This contributes to confusion which, in the target patient, may lead to "craziness". Statements in these families are usually "we" statements, based on the assumption that one person knows exactly what another person thinks and feels. There is little privacy and little autonomy. Who can indeed develop a sturdy self if mother does all the "work" and invalidates the expression of difference in the child? While most of these transactions occur between two people the rest of the family tends to let them go in order not to disturb the peace. The family suffers from acts of multiple collusion. On a motivational level, the family members outside of the dyad may be saving their own skins by sacrificing one member to be the special target.

In extreme cases differences are not only perceived as dangerous but often as "killing" and this produces a belief system that one person's survival depends on another person. Because separation is felt as life endangering, there is little effort to experiment with "little separations". When the actual event of separation occurs, through a child's entering college or marrying, it often leads to a disaster like a suicide attempt, forcing the person who has left to return to the family. The original equilibrium is thus reestablished. The actual events, called the "reality", are often used by the family to explain to themselves and the therapist why they cannot allow separation since indeed the patient by now obliges the family's view of him by acting exactly as "crazy" and irresponsible, as the family has set him up to be. In this manner an unfortunate cycle has been set into motion; the more numerous the failures the more the family is validated in its attempts to keep a member close.

59

Sometimes the reenforcement of such growth-stunting patterns comes not only from the family but also from other systems. Schools may, in an effort to provide education to a school-phobic child, send a home teacher, thus unwittingly playing into the family system. Hospitals may return the improved patient to the very home which maintains his craziness; institutions may work with the patient towards separation without working sufficiently with the family. It is widely recognized that to do so is often counterproductive since the whole burden of change is put on the weakest member who at the same time is also powerful, while the family continues in its accustomed way. In the classroom discussion of this family type, the importance of ecological[7] thinking, the interdependence of various social systems both for assessment as well as treatment purposes is stressed. Instead of ignoring outside systems or dealing with them separately, ecologically oriented family therapists will try to bring the systems together, so that each system's motivational and health potential can be utilized towards the better functioning of the family.

The inclusion of extended kin[8] has opened up another possibility in working with these families. Families are often afraid to engage systems which are too alien. Since the extended family is different but still similar, intervention and help from relatives is more acceptable and can lead to diminishing of the symbiotic bind. Another type of intervention is used through Multi-Family Group Therapy[9] in which various families who have an identified patient (often hospitalized) are treated together in a combination of family and group therapy.

The Depressed-Isolated Family

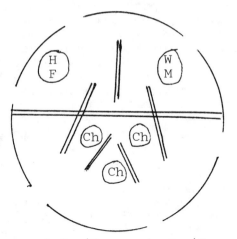

In the depressed family every family member seems separate and few transactions occur among its members.

    This family too is isolated from the outside
world not because it perceives the outside world as
dangerous (Enmeshed Family), nor because it is afraid
of bad influence (Autocratic Family), but because
there is little energy left and it therefore can but
experience few rewards in interchange with the outside
world. This gets noxiously played out within the family where all members are isolated, cacoon-like, as
if they had given up hope to receive from the other
person. The isolation and depression is often covered
up by a lot of busyness some of which is essential to
the functioning of the unit and the emotional surviv-
al-gratification of the individual person. Activities,
however, rather than relationships are the key.

    The Isolated Family displays little emotion and
everything seems muted. It is very different from
the Chaotic Family which is always in motion and
emotional and different from the Enmeshed Family
which operates too closely, in an undifferentiated
way. The students' interest is stimulated by inviting them to speculate what indeed may bring such a
family to our attention. I suggest that the students
imagine what it would be like for them as a child in
a family where everybody is sad and self-absorbed and
where hostility cannot be expressed. We sit still un-

til one student begins to move around and be edgy, another one may begin to giggle. The students' behavior often leads to a possible answer. In such a family a child may be prompted to do something unexpected, wild and fun-filled just to get out of the suffocating silence. To shock may provide some liveliness for himself! Other students become depressed and their bodies begin to ache. Might psychosomatic symptoms be other ways in which people express their feelings or change the cycle? In Family Therapy language, the symptom carrier is seen as the one who brings the family into treatment by giving SOS signals; the one who carries the trouble is also the helper.

Class discussions may stress the difference between treating the depressed person individually or working with the depressed family in such a way as to help them develop other avenues to discharge anger, allow some fun and life to enter their system instead of concentrating on the problem child. His behavior may have, indeed, had the purpose of waking up the family.

There is a great deal of moving back and forth from the discussion of various systems models and interventive modalities, the differences are emphasized, the commonalities stressed and the consequences are considered as to what might be most helpful for a given family. Always, material brought by the students and their behavior in the classroom provides an opening which leads into discussion of a given typology.

REFERENCES

1. Schulman, G.L., "The Single-Parent Family" in Journal of Jewish Communal Services, Summer 1975.

2. _____, "Myths that Intrude on the Adaptation of the Stepfamily" in Social Casework, March 1972,

3. _____, "The Single-Parent Family" in Journal of Jewish Communal Services, Summer 1975.

4. Sheehy, G., Passages, Predictable Crises of Adult Life, New York:Bantam Books, June 1977.

5. Hill, R. and Rodgers, R.H., "The Developmental Approach" in H.T. Christensen (ed.) Handbook of Marriage and the Family, Chicago:Rand McNally 1964.

6. Carter, E.A. and McGoldrick, M., The Family Life Cycle, New York:Gardner Press, Inc. 1980.

7. Auerswald, E.H., "Families, Change and the Ecological Perspective" in Family Process, September 1971.

8. Speck, R.V. et al, "Network Therapy - A Developing Concept" in Family Process, September 1969.

9. Leichter, E. and Schulman, G.L., "Multi-Family Group Therapy; a Multi-Dimensional Approach" in Family Process, March 1974.
   Also: Laqueur, H.P., "General Systems Theory and Multiple Family Therapy" in J.H.Masserman (ed.) Current Psychiatric Therapies, vol. VIII, New York:Grune and Stratton 1968.

CHAPTER V

THE MIDDLE PHASE

Like the middle child, the middle phase in treatment, and in teaching is frequently "forgotten"; as
if it lacked its own unique characteristics, the middle phase does not carry with it the anxious excitement of the beginning phase nor satisfying feeling of
the ending phase. Beginning and ending are more clearly defined - middle is fluid and unclear. The process of the middle phase is characterized by a back
and forth movement of features which could belong to
either phase. All life phenomena which are governed
by time have this characteristic and so has the time-
limited learning process. As a transitory period
the middle phase has no clearly defined starting nor
ending point. Because it lacks drama, it is often
overlooked or treated as unimportant. Awareness occurs only if a special effort is made. In part, this
may account for the mid-life crisis in an individual's
developmental stage; the dramatization of what otherwise may remain unnoticed, the passage of time,
which symbolizes the finiteness of all living organ-
isms.

As a teacher, I deliberately introduce a teaching
structure which helps me and the students to become
aware of this phase that we are in. As in Longfel-
low's poem "I stop between the dark and the daylight".
I stop whatever process we are engaged in and stimulate discussion about where we are, how far we have
gone, and where we may go from here. It is an informal evaluation of the feeling existing in the class,
about the instructor and about the learning process.
It gives the class a chance to move from the doing to
the thinking and feeling and to let come forward
those thoughts and feelings which tend to be buried
in the stream of activities.

Resistance: Force towards Growth

In mid-semester most students have made a beginning with the families with whom they are working.
They have reached some tentative understanding about
family systems and they have translated some of this
knowledge into their work. Yet strangely, just as
some movement has occurred, some stubborn areas of
resistance remain or new ones seem to emerge. Or,
old behavior symptoms may re-emerge. The mood of
hopeful anticipation regarding the magic of this new
modality changes to skepticism and disappointment. In
part, this may be related to the student's knowing and
risking more while becoming more aware of his limitations. In this frame of mind some students are prompted to return to the modality more familiar to them:
namely, to work with individuals or pairs. As these
experiences are brought to class, the students with
help of the instructor grapple with the process and
issues. This usually leads to increasing their understanding of how growth takes place within the family system.

What accounts for "no change", the well-known
"plateau" of the middle phase, "slide back" or the
developments of other areas of noxious behavior in
the mid-phase of family treatment? Explanations usually appear to be related to the two forces of "mor-
phostases[1] and morphogenesis, or the need for "same-
ness or stability" and the need for "change and
growth". If one of these forces is too strong, or too
weak, the system will become dysfunctional, either temporarily or permanently. Since systems have a built-
in corrective factor, a new balance will be found. If
this does not occur, the dysfunctioning will become
repetitive and eventually create pathology. Out of
this dilemma, namely the need to find a functional
balance in a given system during a given time span,
most human problems arise.

Hence, the known phenomenon - the fear of change
(the unknown) is also naturally set into motion when
change occurs, as it does in any effective treatment
process. It may also be the dominant emotion that
makes some systems intensely resistive to change.
Other systems are able to engage in certain kinds of
change while remaining resistive to others. Watzle-
wick[2] differentiates first-order change which consists
merely of an exchange in roles or behavior and second-

order change which is related to a change of rules on which the system is founded. An illustration of the first is, when the heretofore submissive spouse becomes dominant while the dominant one becomes submissive. Second-order changes on the other hand tend to often come about spontaneously, as if a hidden force within the system becomes suddenly freed and may be provided by a person outside of the system, less encumbered by professional methods. These changes cannot always be explained and they sometimes appear "simplistic".

There are various ways of dealing with resistance to change as it occurs in treatment. Some therapists address themselves to the underlying emotions through helping people specify their feelings, thoughts and ideas. Others enable the family to create a situation which is experienced as less frightening, or to help them to detour the experience altogether. Most brief therapy approaches and the increasing popular strategic problem-solving approach, have opened new routes for those families that have little tolerance for anxiety as well as those families that display specific and clearly circumscribed problems. This approach is also useful for any system which is "stuck", including the therapist himself.

Underlying the strategic method is the thought "if you cannot lick them, join them" or to put it more scientifically - to join or even escalate the "resistance". Instead of perceiving resistance as a "hostile" force it is seen as essential in the "back and forth" movement of change. Thus families which do not respond favorably to encouragement or straight tasks often do well with a seemingly "perverse" approach. To give some examples the system can be prescribed: the therapist suggests that the family continue or even accelerate and intensify behavior which is labelled as undesirable. The concept underlying these moves is related to the utilization of ambivalence and the building up of the ego by enabling the person(s) to foresee and be in charge of events so that they feel more in control of a situation. Giving a "paradoxical injunction" is another technique. Paradoxical[3] injunctions are based on the concept that most symptoms have a maintenance function in the system; however as time progresses and the symptom gets intensified the family experiences a dysequilibrium. An example would be when a child's behavior or symptom brings feuding parents together. Or, a child's school

phobia may serve to keep a lonely single parent busy.
Thus the strategically oriented family therapist would
re-label the symptomatic child's role in the system –
calling the child very helpful since he provides his
parents with at least one area of jointness. Would
he give up his behavior, total warfare may rage! In
the second example the child may be congratulated for
sacrificing himself to keep his lonely parent company.

There are other possible developments when change
occurs, which are called the "negative" consequences
of change, although in reality they are positive or
growth inducing: when the child who was the I.P.
ceases to be the scapegoat or relinquishes his symp-
ton the marital conflict which may have been concealed
or not adequately handled because it was detoured
through the child, may now surface. Family therapy
theory postulates that the function of many children
who are scapegoated if symptomatic is precisely to
help parents not to deal with their marital problems.
In cases like this, the change in part of a system
brings about a situation which may be felt as even
more painful than the original problem. Treatment
has brought on a new crisis in which the family has
to choose between alternatives: to go back to the
old way in which a child is being victimized, or to
deal with a new set of problems, i.e., the marital
difficulty. I know of few families that, having once
reached this point of awareness, go back to the old
status quo, even if the marital pair decides not to
re-contract treatment around their difficulties. If
the primary goal, namely the extrication of the child
(the interruption of the transmission of pathology to
yet another generation) has taken place, returning to
the old pattern is really not quite possible, since
the rules of the original game (to have the child be
the stand-in for the marital conflict) are now known
and will, therefore, have lost their effectiveness.
Moreover, few parents consciously want to "use" their
children destructively. Thus, whether such a family
will continue in treatment – with a different focus
and purpose, leave family therapy, or decide to call
the marriage quits, it is obvious that the "other"
problem is nothing but the emergence of the core level
of the family's dysfunctioning.

---

*I.P. = Identified Patient

How to help students to bring a live family

     As time moves on, I urge students to invite a
family for consultation so that they can have a first-
hand experience of the rich possibilities of a consultative family session. This usually sets off an
overt and a covert struggle inasmuch as the proposed
event arouses anxiety on several levels. For one,
most students or beginning trainees, despite having
made a beginning with one or more families,find this
modality still difficult. The proposed structure re-
stimulates thoughts and feelings that are not necessarily related to presenting the family to the class,
but to the idea of family treatment itself. Beyond
these unworked-out feelings the structure itself is
bound to create anxiety since the exposure and the
concomitant voyeuristic components touch upon universal feelings in all of us. The exposure is felt
on two levels: one on behalf of the family and the
other in relation to the student-trainee himself.
The predominant feeling seems to be one of shame, not
for the family having problems or it being a certain
kind of family, but that it will be visible to others.
It is assumed we will judge the family and the therapist unfavorably. This judgment then may ultimately
lead to loss of esteem. This dreaded assumption
creates anxiety and is further intensified by a powerful societal taboo which has to do with privacy.
For a long time the Mental Health profession has
built upon this concept in regard to confidentiality.
This injunction is known to most of us who grew up
professionally in a period of isolated nuclear families surrounded with invisible but powerful boundaries against a judgmental society. Though the
present generation of "groupies" ostentatiously
flaunts this concept and, in some ways, seems to have
overcome some of the myths related to it, remnants of
old traditions continue and get expressed in students'
reactions. This supports the point that cognition is
light-years ahead of emotionality or the irrational
parts of ourselves transmitted from preceding generations and deeply rooted in us.[4]

     The intensity of the class' reaction to the topic
reflects a high degree of fusion[5], so that it becomes
temporarily difficult to ascertain whether the students talk about THE family or themselves, all of
which needs to be brought out and differentiated. It
is not easy at this point for the instructor to stay

related and responsive to the class without merging with the system. This is not unlike what happens to the family therapist in relation to an entrenched family system. The more insecure the instructor is about this particular technique, the more he will be inclined to react, be it by becoming autocratic ("This is how I teach") or by relinquishing his role, dropping the suggestion altogether. The latter may unwittingly give the message to the class that their fears and apprehensions were right in the first place and that the proposal was ill-conceived and dangerous.

Living through this process is exacting. Time and time again I wish I could skip it, envying those institutions which unlike the academic or traditional setting require students to bring families for supervisory and teaching purposes as part of the original contract.* There are various ways in which one can deal with this issue. One can get to the core of the student's feelings re his own family, one can ask the students to close their eyes and imagine how they think their own family (of origin or present) would react to a proposal to be part of such a live consultation. Such fantasy exercises often serve to put the student in touch with his own feelings. Then, these can be separated from the assumed feeling of a given family. The sharing of the fantasy with the group is, itself, strengthening. Students relate a wide variety of situations, thoughts and feelings. They range from the utter dread and fear of catastrophe to more benevolent feelings such as the hope that the audience group will be friendly, supportive and may even come up with helpful suggestions. Fantasies regarding the teacher vary similarly. They range from the omnipotent to the outright destructive. It always makes me shudder to hear in what extreme we perceive the leaders in our profession. Whenever gory examples of a

---

*Many clinics which specialize in family therapy and family therapy teaching institutes operate on the concept that actual observation is preferable to secondhand reporting. They supervise in ways in which the trainee's actual work with the family is observed. This can be done through a one way mirror or in an open solving with the supervisor sitting in the room. Families are informed of this arrangement as part of the treatment contract.

consultant's ineptitude or grandiosity are cited by
the students (some based on actual experience), the
question is raised about the aftermath of the consultation. Interestingly enough, many students do not
know what may have subsequently happened to the family, a fact which often increases their fantasy. The
mere process of concretization: was the family lost
following the viewed consultation, how did the consultant deal with the negatives in the session itself, and most importantly, how did the worker deal
with the family's reaction, demonstrates that this
like other experiences needs to be evaluated in process terms. Any event can be used dynamically and
lead to growth. The message conveyed is that post-
consultation strategy is as important as what precedes
the consultation, and is crucial to the outcome.

Students tend to project into the imaginary family all their assumed fears of what may be going
wrong. The idea that families differ, and thus will
have different reactions and coping patterns and that,
of course, no family will be coerced against its
wishes is usually reassuring to the class. To the
extent that opportunity is given to express doubts
and fears, other voices often come to the fore,
voices that reflect the "other side" conveying trust
and hopefulness and eagerness to partake in an experience which might be helpful and growth promoting.
It is important not to join prematurely the "good"
versus the "bad" children (students) but to permit
the class to live through their own misgivings. As
already indicated, more often than not shifts occur
in which those who had the most vehement doubts about
the idea sometimes become venturesome, whereas others
who were the early promoters of the project, risk
their own doubts. The experience can be likened to
what family therapists are exposed to when they propose a change of structure to a family such as the involvement of members from other systems.

Once some resolution has taken place, questions
and issues are raised which are more related to the
professional rather than the personal Self of the
student-worker. The most typical is related to the
fear that after the consultant's "shining" performance the student's"ineptness" will be known to the
family which will, if not withdraw from treatment, at
least pine for the consultant! Or, if the experience
is felt as a negative one, the student-worker will be
blamed. I usually shock the class by completely a-
greeing that indeed all these things may happen since

71

the consultation is a most potent tool and so are its
consequences. Thus neither the worker nor the consultant can win. If the consultant stimulates change,
the family or some members are bound not to like it,
at least on some level, just like the family will not
like it if nothing happens. Thus all people, client
families are both fearful and desirous of change. So
is the student-worker. If change occurs, he will feel
competitively jealous though glad at the same time.
If no change occurs, he will feel disappointed and
angry while at the same time vindicated by the "limitations" of the consultant who like the student-
worker may feel stymied by the family. In actuality
it is impossible for a consultant and the observing
group not to bring about some change since they are
outsiders and therefore the family and the observing
worker are forced to see and deal with each other differently. Moreover, the consultant's authority and
the knowledge of the uniqueness of the experience enhance the process. It is not uncommon that the observing worker wonders why the consultant is listened
to more than he in regard to a point made by him in
the past. The student-worker in turn has a chance to
see his family from the vantage point of an observer
during the consulting session; and it gives him an
opportunity to become aware of his blind spots.

The second point has to do with the fact that the
consultant is different from the worker not only symbolically but actually. And, family members are also
different from each other. Thus it is virtually impossible for all the members of one family to have
the same reaction vis-à-vis the consultant and the
observing group. Many novice workers tend to take
the reaction of one person, usually the dominant one
in the family, as reflective of the feelings of the
others. This occurs most commonly when the student-
worker's feelings and reactions are similar to those
expressed by the spokesman.

Sometimes the student-worker will be at a loss as
to what to do when a family does not bring up the
topic of the consultation subsequently. This usually
happens in the kind of family which copes by "dis-
connecting" events and feelings (the very same family that may insist that the children's problems
have absolutely nothing to do with their marital difficulties or a recent traumatic event). Such a family will move to "business as usual" and all members
may collude in the "conspiracy of silence" and act as

if "what was, was not". This behavior, like any
other occurring within the family can be looked at as
a statement the family makes about itself and it thus
enhances our understanding of the family and its coping mechanisms. It is essential that the student-
worker does not fall into the trap by joining into
the "conspiracy", but enables the family to re-connect
to the event of the consultation. Once this is done
the family will express their reaction. The student-
worker is advised to deal with the reactions in the
following way:

1) That he receive the message in as much of a
matter of fact way as he can muster. Then he follows
this by inquiring what in the session had felt "worst"
and what "best" (or whatever adjective the person had
used. Some people refer to the session as boring,
others refer to the consultant as hostile or nice or
smart). Thus, an effort needs to be made to concre-
tize and partialize the feelings, something which
often leads to important statements like: "I liked
that she understood me" or "I didn't like it when she
agreed with my son". More often than not statements
like this reflect a person's position in their family
as well as their coping patterns and vulnerable spots,
such as parents of an adolescent who may react to any
display of difference in a personalized way.

2) That he inquire how the rest of the family
sees it. "Who else sees it like mother or didn't like
it like mother", but follow up by insisting that the
person puts his like or dislike into his own words
which often reveals some subtle difference like a
husband not liking "his wife liking something". It is
not uncommon that feelings and thoughts shift in the
process of discussion as they are being seen in a different context. To the extent that the student-worker
allows this process to take place to the fullest, he
has used the consultant as an important bridge between himself and the family which brings the two
closer together and the family can now move on, somewhat changed, as is the student-worker.

It happens frequently that shortly after this
discussion students feel sufficiently confident to
approach their agency and a family for an open consultation. From then on the questions tend to deal
with preparing a family, the format of the consultation, the role of the therapist-student vis-à-vis the
consultant and the timing of the consultation. The

73

suggested approach varies depending, in part, on whether the family is in a beginning process or at a more advanced stage and, perhaps at a plateau; or, whether it is a first "family session" after the student has worked only with an individual. Students are helped to engage the family around this question in such a way that even if a family may decide against the consultation, gains will have been made. For example, in instances when parents hide behind their children claiming that they would object whilst upon a closer look they are the ones who are more fearful. This, in turn, can produce a more realistic self-assessment by the family.

Underlying most of these questions, including those which have to do with the structure, lie important issues such as: autonomy, control and the use of authority. A simple question concerning the desirability to have the interview conducted in an open setting or behind a one-way mirror or one dealing with using audio- or videotape may be channeled in such a way as to aid the class to get "into the skin" of a family, trying to guess how a given family would react to one or another of these possibilities. While the one-way screen* tends to give the family a semblance of privacy and protection and thus approximates more closely the usual interview situation for both the student and the family, the open setting adds the observing group as another dimension to the process. It offers the possibility of an interchange between group and family and can reduce the anxiety which comes from the artificial separation (the presence of something which is known to be but is not seen).

All points made, while reflective of students' attitudes, are likely to be similar to what some families may feel and think. It is often overlooked that the group, because of its anonymity, is like a segment of society at large; thus, some families like the idea of being exposed to the observing group

---

*Since in the strategic school much of the intervention is based upon suggestions coming from a group which observes the family behind the mirror, this technique requires the one-way screen. The Minuchin and Haley approach uses the telephone as a way of supervising the trainee; thus here again the screen serves a specific purpose.

in order to get some feedback and validation and sometimes to establish a coalition. The latter is particularly true when we deal with a lopsided system as in a predominantly female family which is treated by a female therapist and a female consultant leaving the lone male too isolated. In one of the consultations I conducted, such a man, the father of the family, suddenly turned to a male student and in a somewhat desperate voice said, "you understand me, you are a man". Upon occasion I have, as a consultant, turned to a male in the audience and asked him for help, as to how a growing boy may feel. The purpose of such activity is not to accentuate gender differences but to create some balance in a system.

At another consultation, during a point of a great deal of mutual engagement among all the other family members, the youngest child, a five-year old, wandered away from the family to the observing group and got one of the workers to take her onto her lap. The use of the observing group at the end of the session can be another enriching factor when the family and the group are given a chance to respond and interact with each other. The students are prepared for this and are asked to be genuine and responsive rather than pump the family for more information. I have seen students laugh with families and cry with them, share bits of their own lives or make important comments. The family which turns to the class has taken an important step towards the world at large.

Another issue which is bound to come up has to do with the participation of the student therapist in the consultative session. Unlike the role of the co-therapist, which is equal in purpose if not always in status, the student's role in a consultative session is primarily that of observer, albeit an observer with a special status and role with the family. His major contribution precedes and follows the consultation and is of great importance. In the session itself he is the one who ushers the family into the room, lets the family choose their seats and initiates the conversation. Part of the pre-session strategy includes preparing the student for this role. I see him as a bridge between the family and the consultant and it is thus appropriate that it is he who makes the beginning steps which have to do with an acknowledgment of the situation and what it may arouse in all participants. This tends both to lessen the anxiety as well as allowing it to exist. It always shows

how a given family operates in an unusual, novel and
anxiety producing situation and therefore gives an
important clue to how a family handles itself. It is
helpful if the student then moves towards inquiring
where the family sees itself in terms of their process
(I prefer this to a consultant asking what is troubl-
ing the family, or what they see as their problem because letting the student-worker do it validates the
fact that the family is in a treatment process with
him and in all likelihood has been engaged and may
have begun to change).

I see the consultation as a link in a chain, so
that in the beginning as well as in the end of the
consultation I like to emphasize the role of the
worker while during the major portion of the consultation it is the consultant who conducts the session;
a fact the worker prepared the family for. Of course,
there is no hard, fast rule concerning the quantity
or quality of the student's participation. However,
in the pre-consultation strategy I emphasize that
there are some areas where I absolutely depend on the
student. For example, at certain points he can operate as "reality carrier" both if the family appears
to behave very differently from their usual "self" or
when the consultant is unable to know how much change
has already occurred. Comments such as: "I have
never seen the family quite so formal" gives the consultant a clue as to the degree of stress the family
is under. Or, a worker may state in response to the
consultant's remark about the lack of participation
of a member, i.e., "You should have seen Johnny a few
weeks ago when he didn't even say a word and sat with
his head turned against the wall". Not only are such
remarks experienced by the family as supportive, they
also indicate to the consultant how much the family
has changed. Throughout the consultation, due to the
fact that the worker is temporarily relieved of his
role, he can observe the family transactions in a
different way and can see how the family transacts
with a different system (the consultant). If he perceives a situation different from the consultant, he
is urged in the pre-consultation strategy to voice
his difference. Such articulation is very beneficial,
it may lend needed support to one member of the family, or it may pinpoint a student-worker's tendency
to protect a member in an emerging maneuver and this
phenomenon can be dealt with as can differences in
perception between the student-worker and the consultant. All of this serves as a good model for the
family as to how to deal with differences, etc. with-

out the loss of status.

The worker's presence in spite of the fact that he relinquishes his leadership by design, gives the family a sense of security and continuity. The interplay between the student-worker and the consultant is a somewhat paradoxical one. In one sense the consultant is clearly in a leadership position, yet he will at times turn to the worker as the one truly knowledgeable about the family. In a way both the worker and the consultant are of and out of the system, now in coalition with each other, now in alliance with the family, i.e., sometimes doers, sometimes observers.

The pre-consultation discussion often brings out misunderstandings on the part of the students, discussion of which tends to clarify the process and to decrease some of the anxiety. The live interview itself will be discussed in a separate chapter. The reader, at this point, will need to imagine that a live consultation has already taken place and that the family has just left the room. I consider it important that the class stay together for a few moments to share their sense of excitement and be as "reactive" as possible. Comments like: "Are you always as active" or "I felt so sad for the woman", "Why have you left the little girl out so much" reflect and communicate what a student is struck by. It may convey relief, pain, anger or other feelings. I try to hear and receive the overt and not so overt but add that there will be ample time in the next class session to talk about their feelings and observations in greater detail. This debriefing is somewhat akin to what I try to do at the end of the consultation with the family and what should be done in any group meeting which engendered strong feelings and thinking reactions.

When I first began teaching I was struck by the contrast a week later when the class met again. The "high" which existed so noticeably immediately after the consultation was gone and had been replaced by a more sober mood. At times it is even hard to get the process going. Furthermore, if the consultant has a lot of narcissistic investment in positive feedback from the students his disappointment and puzzlement will be great. There are probably many things which are set into motion which may account for this phenomenon: first and foremost, the natural cyclical

swing from euphoria to depression, from emotional
overflow to the cognitive state. Feelings which may
be felt as less acceptable may be submerged. With
some encouragement and a little patience however,
feelings and opinions get expressed. Comments range
from the highly subjective idiosyncratic, from too
much praise to too much disapproval, from focusing on
just one sub-system, a person, to observations that
are accurate but indicative of only one piece and
are not looked upon in its context. The most frequent
criticism directed against me as the consultant has to
do with the amount of work (activity) I do. "Are you
always as active in a family even if it were your own,
in private practice?" "You must have been exhausted".
These types of feedback reveal either a real difference between the passive "listening and waiting" attitude of the traditional individual therapist or some
fear that the student will be expected to put in as
much exertion and labor. I usually emphasize that
being an attentive observer who is constantly thwarted
by his inclination to move into the situation itself,
may be more strenuous than being the doer. In trying
to get to the meta message, the feeling behind the
overt statement, I try to convey acceptance of the
student's right not to like what I have done, while at
the same time suggesting that he pay attention to both
the family's response to my activity and also to the
purpose I had in mind. For instance, the need to organize and provide leadership for a chaotic leaderless
family. This may be giving priority to what the student rightfully perceives as the need of a mother to
hold the consultant exclusively in the orbit of her
attention. Thus, while allowing this flow I, as the
teacher, am treading a thin line between encouraging
expressions from the students and guiding them towards
some conceptualization of what they have seen. The
teacher should help them describe the family and system, to identify the family patterns and the process
they are engaged in with each other and the therapeutic system. Students are challenged to "prove" their
hunches and hypotheses on the basis of what they observed in a person, in a dyad and within the whole
family group. When their focus of interest is on a
sub-group, usually the most active, dramatic one, they
are asked to remember what the rest of the family did
during this period. In this way the importance of the
so easily overlooked "non-actors" is stressed as another vital clue to understanding the family system.
For example, the mother's contented look when the son
challenged his father. Students are alerted to the

importance of the context of a transaction or action
as well as to the timing.

An example of the above is the sudden bad behavior of a child in a session which may be preceded by
the first attempt on the part of the spouses to talk
about things important to them. The child's action
is both a way to interrupt the transaction as well as
to connote his own anxiety. Wherever possible, the
aim is to substitute linear thinking with cyclical,
systems thinking. The difference between spontaneous
behavior initiated in the family itself versus behavior in response to a therapeutic intervention is important to assess, both diagnostically and prognosti-
cally. It is a way to determine directions of movement and the points of vulnerability of the system.
In the consultation which will be described in the
following chapter, the consultant re-arranged the
seating in such a way that the father had to deal with
his youngest daughter; this left the mother, who had
been kept busy by the little girl, isolated from the
rest of the family. Suddenly, the adolescent son who
happened to be the problem child and was labeled as
selfish and not a bit interested in the family, moved
his chair close to his mother's and put his arms a-
round her. What a telling family sequence! It would
neither be sufficiently described by labeling the mother-son behavior as oedipal or the father as passive
because he needed to be helped to move to his daughter
or, worse yet, as just "conforming to the therapist's
move" thus devaluating his behavior because it was
not fully self-engendered. Sequences like this, when
properly understood, show trainees not only what is,
but what is possible in a family if change occurs -
change of behavior and structure which has profound
impact on feelings and attitudes in the family.

Since first impressions are potent and tend to
stay ingrained in the observer, it is important to
help the student to "move with the family", so that
the likelihood of labeling is decreased and things
are viewed in transactional rather than in predominantly intrapsychic terms. For instance, the father
who tends to be unfeeling and lecturing to his son
while gentle to his little daughter is likely to be
labeled as an unfeeling intellectualizer. How much
more meaningful if he were described as a person who
responds to his son in one way and to his daughter in
another way. Furthermore, this behavior can become
more comprehensive when one sees it within the con-

text of a mother-son coalition to which the father has no access. Or, instead of labeling a man passive it can be noted that while usually silent, possibly in response to his wife's contemptuous attitude, at one point he gave his opinion.

Trainees sometimes get discouraged when, after a meaningful interview, the last remark on the part of a family member is negative. Like first impressions, these last words tend to take on a powerful meaning and stick in our minds. To view such remarks as a part rather than the whole, in the context of an ending experience is vital. Words are imbued with magic and are frequently given more "oomph" in our profession than the total behavior in itself. Should a statement of a sullen adolescent that he thinks little of the session and doesn't care what happens to his family be trusted more than his shaking hands with the therapist upon leaving? The latter may be a warm gesture in response to positive comments the therapist made about him during the session.

These things are discussed after the live family interview. This leaves the class understanding the live session differently and in a more integrated way. Greater comprehension is made possible by means of a process which tends to fuse feelings and cognition into a whole. It also gives the instructor a pretty accurate picture as to where his class is. A considerable amount of time is devoted to this dialogue with the students. References to the experience itself continue for the remainder of the semester. As will be seen in another chapter, this may become one of the most valuable episodes in the total learning process.

The Trainee's Special Role

However, I consider my most important task in the post-session interview to focus on the student-worker whose job it is to continue to work with the family. It is the only time in the entire semester that I will deliberately put the need of one individual before the need of the group. The reason for this is obvious, it lies not only in the fact that the student has taken special pains to bring the family to the class, but his very action requires special attention and help. His position, different from the rest of the class, is not only to learn from the ex-

80

perience and utilize this knowledge at a later point,
but also it is he who will have to deal with the family and face the music! Whether dealt with earlier or
not, the student's competitive and critical feelings
need to surface lest they be obstacles in his future
dealings with the family. The expression of feelings
alone, of course, is not sufficient. The worker-student has to be provided with tools for dealing with
the family's reactions. Some of these reactions are
predictable in the light of a given family. Some are
not, and may occur later in the form of indirect actions which the student needs to be alerted to.

In one such consultation, the husband's murderous
rage in response to his wife's infidelity had finally
come out. This was responded to as better than the
severe depression into which he had sunk for an entire year. The consultant, while mindful of the potential for violence, had tested how much self-control
the man had and a more meaningful marital interchange
developed. However, upon the family's return home,
and in response to a slight provocation on the part
of the wife, this husband beat his wife for the first
time. The worker was upset and angry with the consultant who had been instrumental in eliciting this
material, which had both gotten beyond the depression
and also re-directed the man's rage to the wife instead harboring the homicidal fantasy towards his
wife's former lover. The worker-student had, understandably, taken the wife's side. He had come back
to class intent on showing the consultant what a bull
the man was. In his identification with the woman and
revulsion to physical violence he had overlooked to
see the violent action as part of a process. As this
became clarified the student was able to handle the
marital difficulty by enabling the couple to come to
grips with a "past event".

In view of the fact that students often do not
have supervision available in family therapy cases,
I offer myself, if necessary, to the student as an
individual consultant if the class discussion does
not prove to be sufficient. I consider this a legit-
imate use of my time. I have a certain responsibility
to the family that was brought in for consultation.

Once the student realizes that he will not be
left alone, it is remarkable how resourceful he becomes. In one live class consultation that coincided
with the student's leaving the agency at the end of

the semester another student who had secured employment at the same agency was approached by the first
student and agreed to accept the case - a plan that
they subsequently sold to the agency! Due to this,
the benefits of the consultation and the continuity
of the process were insured. Only once, in the author's long experience as a consultant did it happen
that a family insisted, after the student left at the
end of the semester, on being treated by me (the consultant) privately. It required a great deal of cooperation between the agency and myself to work out
a suitable plan acceptable to the family. The reason for this family's despair was less related to
the consultation than to the fact that this family
had been handed down from worker to worker which increased their sense of abandonment. However, this
sense of abandonment had not been dealt with sufficiently.

After the Consultation

The return to "work as usual" after the live interview has its difficulties. In general, there is a
lot of excitement engendered by this experience and
there is considerable push to get into the act. Several students now are ready to offer families for
such an experience. Since I am usually not able to
accomodate more than two in one semester, some may be
turned down. In the chapter on training groups I will
discuss the difference existing in the academic one-
semester situation and longer-term training programs
in agencies. Timing is another factor inasmuch as I
never interview a live family during the last two
class sessions because termination with the group
needs to be given priority. Thus, the scarcity of
live case material in the earlier period makes way
for an ever-increasing flow, all of which means that
we have passed a crisis successfully and that greater
trust is being established.

The move now is more to selectivity of case material. This means that I give priority to cases
that have content material with which I have not dealt
with thus far, such as the impact other systems have
upon the nuclear family, cultural and racial aspects
or families with unusual symptoms. Almost, though not
of equal importance, in my opinion, is an attempt to
get those students involved who thus far have tended
to keep in the background. This can be done by being

more reponsive to non-verbal clues, timid attempts to
say something that may get drowned out by the more
vociferous in the group or some focus on the phenomenon of overt non-participation itself. One can use
this by asking what the silent students may be telling the group. This generally brings some movement
in the desired direction, though it is by no means
foolproof and there are always some students who
choose to learn in a most "private" way. It has become obvious in the students' criticisms of me that
some experience my efforts as not being sufficient.
The chapter on student types will deal with this.

Some instructors who are less experienced clinicians will use videotapes of other therapists. In
the rare case where students have not been able to
bring a live family to my class, I use at least one
videotape in which I am the consultant clinician, in
order to give students as much of a sense as possible
how I operate in an interviewing situation. Watching
a videotape gives the class an advantage to study
some of the minutiae of the family and therapeutic
process. The showing can be interrupted at any point;
certain moves can be discussed at the moment they
occur, parts can be replayed. distortions, at least
some, can be corrected or questioned. This is not to
be confused with the previously mentioned showing of
videotapes introducing other therapists so that alternate types of family therapy can be seen. While the
advantage of showing a videotape is obvious, the live
interview gives the students an opportunity to truly
participate in the process in a way that can never be
duplicated by canned material. In the live situation
the painstaking preparation of the group and the actual experience of watching a live family, with the
elements of the unknown that are a genuine binder between the therapist, the consultant, the class and
the family, is quite unique. The group is involved
in the original preparation and post event strategy.
Yet, more than anything else, watching a live family
touches upon the deep emotions available in all individuals and groups. It is amazing how much the group
shares in the anxiety and the suspense that comes
from the unpredictability of life itself. Moreover,
it places the consultant in a less hierarchical position since the group knows qite well that he too
exposes himself. On a technical level, the limitations of a tape, including the narrowness of the field
of vision, are numerous. Above all, the fact that it
is seen through the lens of another person, the cam-

eraman. Videotapes are, at best, a filtered version
of reality.

The Middle Phase in treatment and in teaching
gradually flows into and perhaps merges with the
first awareness of the closeness of the ending. This
awareness is, at best, dim; but it will, later in
the ending phase, become more intense and clear.

REFERENCES

1. Speer, D., "Family Systems: Morphostasis and
   Morphogenesis, or is Homeostasis Enough?" in
   Family Process, September 1970.

2. Watzlawick, P., Weakland, J.H., and Fisch, R.,
   Change: Principles of Problem Formulation and
   Problem Resolution, New York:Norton 1974.

3. Papp, P., "The Greek Chorus and Other Techniques
   of Paradoxical Therapy" in Family Process, March
   1980.

4. Halleck, S., "Family Therapy and Social Change" in
   Social Casework, October 1976.

5. Bowen, M.. "Theory in the Practice of Psychotherapy" in Family Therapy, Guerin, P.J.,Jr.(ed.),
   New York:Gardner Press 1976. (Refers to the
   fact that if the cognitive faculty gets overwhelmed by the feeling faculty objectivity gets
   reduced).

CHAPTER VI

THE DEMONSTRATION INTERVIEW

The demonstration interview has become one of the standard teaching devices in the field of family therapy. It is a remarkable learning tool.

In the past the practice of presenting a patient in the auditorium of a psychiatric hospital was frowned upon by the rest of the mental health profession. It was seen as exploitative, lacking in human dignity and a violation of a patient's right to privacy. As in a self-fulfilling prophecy, the circumstances around which such interviews usually took place served to confirm people's worst fears. The psychiatric patient was presented to a huge audience of eager spectators (students) and was asked to tell about his "symptoms". The patient frequently obliged and described with gusto some of the irrational aspects of his condition. Since this profession was symptom- and illness-related, little attempt was made to get to the healthy parts of the person or to the environment within which he experienced these symptoms. The willingness of some of the patients to "cooperate" can be attributed less to their being disconnected from reality, than to their welcoming an opportunity to either get some attention, have a break from the monotony of their hospital life, or to bring their plight to the attention of the world!

Another type of demonstration interview was, and still is, used in certain psychiatric hospitals at the time of "evaluation", often in preparation to the patient being discharged. Like a student who has to pass a most difficult examination, the "rite of admission to the world of sanity", though less bizarre than the one cited earlier, may be even more anxiety arousing. The impression the patient makes on his audience may lead to his discharge or at least to gaining some privileges. While the questioning psy-

85

chiatrist was often kind and related, the hierarchical
components of the situation and its "life and death"
quality are always present. In the classroom the atmosphere is completely different. The students are
neither judges, helpers, nor adversaries, but are re-
presentatives and therefore symbols of the world at
large. An example of this difference may be seen in
a recent demonstration session which a single parent
family, consisting of a mother and her three children.
The family had been broken up several years ago due
to the mother's temporary neglect of her very young
children. The mother, under the influence of liquor
(accompanied by her second husband, the father of the
youngest child) had left the children unattended for
two full days. The children were put into a foster
home and were only returned to the mother after she
separated from her second husband, given up drinking
and for all intents and purposes had become practically ascetic, keeping away from life's temptations
and pleasures. Needless to say, this family encountered difficulties when the oldest daughter became an
adolescent and began to act in ways reminiscent of
the mother's past behavior. In the pre-consultation
discussion I encouraged the class to tell the woman
directly what they were thinking - that they were
"forgiving" of this mother's past "sins" and as "mes-
sengers" on behalf of the adult world were giving her
the right to "lead her own life". She could learn to
balance responsibility as a mother while at the same
time operating as an adult responding to her own
needs. According to plan, the interchange between
the group and the woman in front of her children took
place. She first did not believe that anybody, let
alone these middle-class professionals, had any understanding, or sympathy, for what prompted her to leave
her children. The disbelief changed to belief and
finally outright joy when she heard repeatedly from
various students, especially the older ones, that
they would want her to not only devote herself to mo-
therhood but also to becoming a person in her own
right.

There is, in my opinion, no one specific family
suitable for consultation, though consultants may
have their preferences[1]. Exposure to all kinds of
families and situations is particularly important
when teaching social work students who rarely have
the luxury to select certain kinds of families; more
often than not they are exposed to families in the
midst of a crisis or to those who seem "unmotivated

and unwilling" or have an atypical structure. I follow these steps for all demonstration interviews:

     1.   Preparation of the family
     2.   Pre-consultation strategy with the students
     3.   The interview in the classroom
     4.   Post-interview class discussion.

This will now be illustrated in detail using the case
of the "P" family:

1.   PREPARATION OF THE FAMILY

When Mr. A. a student with some prior experience
mentioned his interest to bring the P family to class,
it was suggested that he tell the family that participation in a demonstration consultation might benefit
both the family and the therapist. He was asked to
describe to the family in simple terms the setting
and the format in which the interview would take
place, and then give the family ample opportunity to
react and raise questions which needed to be responded to factually, while recognizing the underlying
feelings. No member would be allowed to "hide" behind the other, yet as with other vital treatment decisions, the parents should be asked to be the final
decision makers. The quality and form of the participation however, would be left to each individual.
(Adolescents often state that they will come, but will
not speak. No issue is to be made regarding such a
statement, which often only means that the adolescent
expects to be scapegoated). On the other hand students are warned against too ready acceptance of
"family enthusiasm", since some families in their eagerness to please say "yes" prematurely. If this is
so, then "second thoughts" tend to appear. Students
are, therefore, encouraged to allow the family time
to talk the matter over with each other, and to deal
with the ambivalent feelings which usually come out
eventually.

Mr. A. seemed comfortable with the thought of
preparing the family; the only major issue revolved
around the question of the grandparents' participation in the session in view of the fact that the therapist had already involved them and some progress
seemed to have been made in this area. The consultant teacher felt that the family could benefit either
way, but since she wanted to strengthen the new con-

stellation (the nuclear family) in order to emphasize the boundaries of the family, she indicated a slight preference to see the immediate family.

2. PRE-CONSULTATION STRATEGY WITH THE STUDENTS

Once the family had agreed to come the student shared the following details with the class. He had had only four family sessions thus far since he began working with the family and felt that some progress had been made. He wanted, however, some confirmation of his assessment, and some direction for the future. The P family consisted of Mr. P (Harry), middle-aged, his two children from his first marriage, Leslie 17, and Fred 14, as well as his second wife Florence (somewhat younger and attractive), and Mary, their five-year old daughter (from this second marriage). The P's had been married for 11 years. Mr. P's first wife had died when Fred was only 2 years old and Mrs. P's first marriage had ended in divorce when her son Paul, now 21, was a tiny boy. While he had orig-inally lived with the P's, Paul was now living with a paternal uncle and aunt and was alleged to be in-volved with drugs. Mr. P's parents played an impor-tant role in the family. These grandparents were said to be intrusive, overprotective of Fred, and very critical of Mrs. P.

The family was referred for family counseling to the agency, where the student was placed, after a frustrating contact on the part of the protective agency to which Fred had originally been referred by the school. He had been a truant and unruly at school. The family considered his behavior "impos-sible". They described him as heartless and selfish, revealing that he had once molested his half-sister, Mary. A psychological study confirmed the bleak pic-ture, labeling Fred a "sociopath". Fred had been worked with individually, but his worker reported that he had not been able to establish any rapport with the boy.

The student, in his initial work with the family, had concentrated on reducing their preoccupation with Fred and had, correctly in my opinion, dealt with the grandparents' over-involvement in the family. He in-vited the grandparents to participate in sessions that revealed their alliance with Mr. P, their son (over-involved and enmeshed family members usually

like to participate in sessions; in fact, they are
often resentful of not being asked to do so). As the
involvement decreased, a rather strong marital conflict emerged, something which the family had been
aware of but in no way connected to Fred's difficulties.

In the strategic session with the class, we focused on the structure of the family and its influence
on the family patterns, attitudes and interactions,
as well as the possible relationship to the problem
child. We noted what was known and what had to be
further explored. We started out by showing on the
blackboard the present constellation and the other
currently involved systems as imagined by ourselves:

Diagram I

11 years married

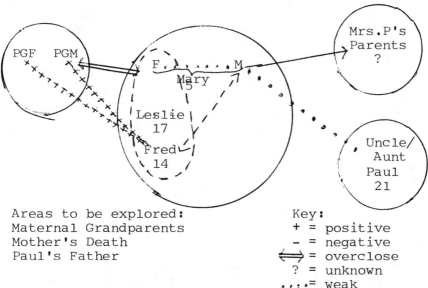

Areas to be explored: Key:
Maternal Grandparents   + = positive
Mother's Death   - = negative
Paul's Father   ⟺ = overclose
                      ? = unknown
                   ....= weak

We were certain, on the basis of the student's report that the paternal grandparents played, at least
in part, a noxious role through their over-investment
and negative relationship with their daughter-in-law,
the stepmother. (This puzzled us somewhat, although
this kind of attitude can be expected if the maternal
grandparents /the parents of the deceased spouse/ had
been around, since there is usually a residue of resentment in the case of a dead child /in this case

their daughter⎦ against the surviving spouse and often also against her replacement ⎣the stepmother⎦. In such a case, the grandparents tend to either draw the grandchildren into their orbit or detach themselves from them. This may well have occurred in this family, although we never had a chance to clarify this in the consultation). The evidence was that the paternal grandparents never relinquished their protective or infantilizing role in relation to Mr.P. This was confirmed in the consultation by the fact that the grandparents favored Fred, which, of course, had quite an impact on the sibling system and may have intensified Fred's having become the scapegoat in this family.

There was considerable evidence of marital dysfunctioning. This frequently exists when two systems "wed" but the wedding never quite gets consummated. The marriage remains weak and the step-parent is either under- or overused. The latter occurs more often in cases of stepmothers who tend to get saddled with extra responsibilities without receiving the full backing of their husbands, the father of the children. Stepfathers, in contrast, often stay on the periphery of the family action, feel mildly resentful about the situation and are in some bind, since they are often accused of lacking "interest and affection" while at the same time they are not permitted to take on the paternal prerogatives.

There was no information about Paul's relationship to his mother, or her family of origin, both of which are areas that are useful to explore in the course of treatment. The class and I hypothesized that whatever the reasons for Fred being the scapegoat, Mrs. P may well have resented her husband's son who, contrary to her own son, was allowed to stay in the family. We reiterated that we did not know the circumstances of Paul's exit but speculated that Mary was planned to cement a shaky marriage and may have been the father's peace offering to his wife for giving up Paul. Speculations of this sort need to be clearly labeled and if not confirmed in further work with the family they need to be discarded. There was certain evidence that Fred had been difficult for a long period of time and we were interested in having the family help us to figure this out. We also wondered whether the developmental state of Fred's adolescence did not intensify whatever problem he had. The fact that there was some incestual sex play be-

tween Fred and his half-sister Mary, indicated some
problem in sexuality in the family. This occurs in
weak marital relationships, but more frequently in
reconstituted families in which the incest taboo is
weaker between those not bonded through blood. The
onset of adolescence would be more troublesome for
any child who carried the scapegoating role and
whose impulse control is not well developed. Thus,
some exploration about Fred's role in the family was
planned though not in too direct a way. This was in
line with my tendency not to focus on the problem
child (or any other overt problem in the family) but
rather to pay attention to other dysfunctioning areas
in the family. There was some question regarding
the pros and cons of involving the grandparents in
this particular session; in view of the fact that
this area had been productively worked on by the
students, we thought that seeing the nuclear family
would have advantages. Before we could make a decision the grandparents had departed on a trip!

It was decided that the strategy for the consultative session would focus on the following issues:

a. The discomfort of the strange setting
b. The changes thus far
c. Exploration of particular areas which
    appeared important and had thus far not
    been clarified, especially the area sur-
    rounding the natural mother's death and
    Paul's expulsion
d. The role of the stepmother and how the
    family dealt with this phenomenon, in-
    cluding the mythology usually attached
    to this role.

The way families deal with stepmothers depends
largely on whether the father has been the main caretaker of his children or whether he has delegated the
care of the children to other people. In the first
case the stepmother encounters similar difficulties
as stepfathers do; they tend to be viewed as outsiders who have few rights vis-à-vis the children and
they are in a low power position in the family. In
the latter case which turned out to be the situation
in the P family, the father tends to "dump" the children on the stepmother, which leaves her in an overburdened yet not sufficiently supported position.
(Some women feel that they are being chosen not as
wives, but as mothers). In both instances the per-

91

ception of the stepmother on the part of family members and society at large is colored by the mythology surrounding the notion of stepmotherhood as "bad, mean and wicked."[2]

    e.   The marital relationship
    f.   The role of the father in relation to his children with the goal of unburdening the stepmother
    g.   Clues on how Fred became the problem child and what in the family served to maintain him in this role.

I suggest to the students that they watch how this plan is executed, which areas are dropped, which were developed and what other directions were being followed. Before the family is ushered in by the student worker, I arrange the room in the following way: chairs for all family members (even the missing ones, if appropriate), the student worker and the consultant are arranged in a semi-circle. The observing group of students faces the family ·with some distance between them and the family. Their seats are arranged much like in an amphitheater, in a semi-circle. The family should have easy access to their seats. I request that the observers do not take notes. The selection of chairs by family members occasionally gives important clues regarding its alliances, distance, and position in the family (an outsider or the central member). I have noticed that the person who takes the central, middle position, the one facing the audience is a person who is not timid, who has some expectation that the world will be on his side. The two most protected seats which are usually turned more to the family and less to the audience are generally left free for the therapists. Whatever the unconscious reasons, I like to believe that the family on some level is sensitive to the need of the therapist, who is exposed to the group. I, for one, am grateful for this arrangement!

3.   THE DEMONSTRATION INTERVIEW: "THE FAMILY THAT FORGOT TO MOURN"

This report of the interview is highly condensed but follows the actual process. As the P family entered and tried to make its way passed the observing group, there was a lot of commotion and scrambling for positions. Mother finally maneuvered to

take the lead. She entered first, mumbling "why do
I always have to be first?". This theme, namely the
mother's grudging acceptance of leadership in the
family with all its members in collusion to keep it
that way, remained one of the major themes in the session. The consultant referred to it in various ways,
finally, as we shall see, changing the structure so
that the accustomed way was blocked. A major thought
behind this was related to the fact that the family
needed to move from the "bad and overworked stepmother" to a different balance. The theme of discomfort
about the setting was touched upon, though not totally developed. Then the family, first the mother and
then the father, spontaneously referred to a change.
- Mr. P had loosened his involvement with his parents,
which Mrs. P had noted with pleasure. This was acknowledged and denied at the same time. The couple
directed itself to me, the consultant, and was verbally and then structurally directed through changing
seats to talk to each other instead of about each
other. (Responses to this maneuver as well as the
acknowledgement of the noxious role of the grandparents indicated the degree to which the family had allowed the student worker to enter the system and to
begin to make changes. Student workers often wonder
how a consultant can judge whether the family has
made progress if it is not articulated by the family.
There are many non-verbal clues and other indications
that generally give an accurate picture about a family's relationship to their worker and reflect what a
family has learned thus far). The theme of the stepmother was introduced by the consultant after inquiring how Mrs. P (Florence) was called by the children.
Each of the children was asked directly (including
little Mary). The consultant used the word "stepmother" in a deliberate attempt to "untaboo" the taboo.
While initially not picked up, Mrs. P finally explod-
ed and angrily said to the consultant that she disliked
being called by this name. She then proceeded to explain how hard being a stepmother had been for her,
due to her in-laws' extremely negative attitude,
their influence on Fred - who, when she said this defended his grandparents - symbolized by the grandmother's momentous statement that when she got married
to Mr. P "the children would have been better off
dead", and last but not least the fact that her husband never stood up for her against his parents'
snide remarks. Instead, he withdrew increasingly and
left her to do "all the dirty work". It turned out
that, due to disgust, she had walked out on the fam-

ily at various occasions, but always returned when her husband pleaded with her to come back. Her anger at the state of affairs and her hurt about not being appreciated was divided between her husband and Fred, who, however, became increasingly the target due to his bad behavior. (The consultant, thinking in systemic terms thought that Fred's bad behavior may have been a "helpful" move to protect his father or the marriage, but also that other "reasons" may have contributed to his position: like the expulsion of the stepmother's son and the closeness of the paternal grandparents to him.)

After restating the difficulty of Florence's role and the fragility of the marriage, I moved to get the father into a more central position. I inquired about the children with regard to their father. This, somewhat unexpectedly, led to an interchange in the sibling sub-system. Brother and sister had so far totally ignored each other (a fact the consultant had noticed silently, thinking that this dyad needed to be strengthened). Leslie first scapegoated Fred (thus allying herself with the stepmother as well as reflecting the system) but then picked up on the theme of change and mentioned that Fred recently seemed less "callous" to her. Fred then responded that this was natural since she was less bossy (an example of the typical circular nature of dyadic transactions). This led to a rather warm interchange between the siblings in which their underlying longing to be loved and appreciated by the other emerged. This theme was later extended to the marital relationship.

It was obvious that Mr. P needed more direct help to get out of his immobile position. Therefore, I directed the discussion to Fred and his father, picking up on the fact that mother in this family was overburdened. I proposed to change this by giving Mr. P a chance "right now" to do something differently, namely helping his wife with little Mary. (Mary had so far either been sitting on her mother's lap or sticking very closely to her, holding on to her). Mr. P hesitated and wondered aloud how Mary would react to an invitation to come to him, since she, he said, always came to mother except when he horseplayed with her. (I noted silently that Mrs. P neither helped nor obstructed her move). She then encouraged her somewhat reluctant husband to help Mary to come to him. He finally stretched out his arms, beckoning the child. Mary slowly got up, looked back at her mother to check with her and, when the latter nodded, she went close to her father. He pulled her onto his lap where she first sat stiffly. However, something quite dramatic occurred at the point when Mary and her father had relaxed with each other and mother had been left isolated.

Diagram II

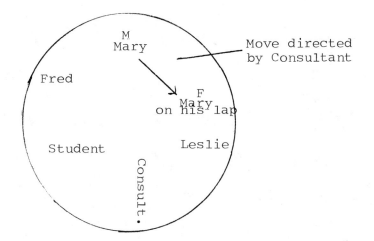

Suddenly and even before I was aware of Florence's isolated position, Fred picked up his chair and moved closer to his stepmother! She did not move away, but smiled. He then put his arms around her shoulders! (See Diagram III)

Diagram III

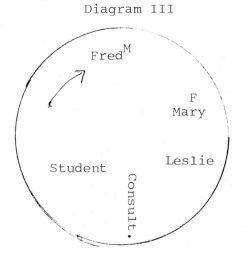

Fred confronted his father after moving back to his original seat from which he could face his father directly. In past interviews he had only spoken in monosyllables and never spontaneously; now he began to attack his father. The picture that emerged, not incidentally, disputed by the family, was one of the grandparents' caring for the children after Fred's mother's death. As a baby, Fred became extremely spoiled. Interrupting Fred's account, Leslie bitterly caricatured her grandmother's fussing over Fred while she herself was admonished to act as the reasonable older sister. Small wonder then that when Florence entered the family scene it was Leslie not Fred who welcomed her. Leslie recalled how her future stepmother read them bedtime stories and brought goodies even prior to her entering the household. Florence smiled when she heard Leslie's account and stated that she never knew that Leslie remembered those times. Though never articulated, it was obvious from this account why Leslie had welcomed and Fred had fought the stepmother's joining the family. Fred apparently lost the protection of his grandmother and it would not be surprising if some of the resentment existing between stepmother and grandmother may have revolved around their differences in treating the children. Of course, Fred did not let his sister dwell on her memories too extensively, but accused his father of marrying so quickly and never, not even once, referring to their mother. The father had been well-meaning but his attempt to disconnect the children from their roots was ill-fated.

Moreover, Fred was often sent to the basement because his father found him difficult and very "silly". "Why did you do this?" Fred asked and his father lamely defended himself, putting the blame, as always, back onto Fred's behavior. However, Fred confronted his father with evidence of the father's, not his, inappropriate behavior: "how silly can a 4-5-year old be or what crimes could I have committed?" Further, it is likely that Harry mistakenly thought that Florence would object to his ever mentioning his first wife, in addition to his general tendency to deal with painful matters by merely avoiding them. Later in the interview Fred reproached his father by saying that even now when he turns to him for sexual information the father just brushes him off with embarrassed silence or admonishes him to wait until he is more grown up. My comments throughout were either to confirm a point, to show some connections or to clarify, and stressing always what needs to change. Comments in Florence's and Fred's Direction often were put thusly: "after all it is not all his fault; but things were screwed up in the family". Encouraged by Fred's stand, Leslie joined her brother and reminded her father in a choked-up voice that she had for years begged him to take her to visit her mother's grave and that he had always found an excuse not to do so. Fred then echoed the wish of his sister. The emergence of this genuine sibling alliance was gratifying to see.

It was clear that there was a great deal of unfinished business and mourning to do: I proposed that they make a plan around the cemetery visit in the session. While the father did not like the idea, he yielded to the joint pressure of the children and me, who called it most urgent. I enabled the triad to make detailed plans about the visit. Somewhere in the discussion Florence said how well she understood the children's feelings since she too had lost a parent, her father, when she was but a few months old. At another juncture, when Fred confronted his father with the almost brutal behavior he displayed toward him (excluding him from family activities) Florence said that this was one of the reasons that her son Paul left the house after only staying for a few years. I, while considering the issue of the "lost" son an important and powerful one, still chose to pursue the father-child confrontation, leaving the other for another time.

Throughout the session the marital difficulty was worked on directly and indirectly. As the father's position was made more central the stepmother's position became less so. Similarly, as Mr. P achieved some degree of separation their conflict was dealt with directly rather than detoured through involving Mr. P's parents or Mr. P's children. Thus, when the focus moved toward direct exchange between the couple, the "children" were symbolically extricated (through change of the seating arrangements) and Mr. and Mrs. P were encouraged to talk about their relationship which, as was evident, had been extremely rocky and mutually dissatisfying. Florence and Harry were asked to state what they wanted from each other. As could be expected Florence quite aggressively demanded from her husband more "giving" in concrete and emotional terms. Harry defended himself with a typical passive stance, at which point Fred intervened

97

on the side of his stepmother, pleading with his father "to join her in the kitchen and talk to her instead of withdrawing behind TV". The consultant
thanked Fred for his good suggestion, but insisted
that the issue was between husband and wife and could
only be resolved by them. (The consultant pointed out
to the students in the post-demonstration class how
essential it was for Fred's development to have his
parents manage better as a couple, or at least stay
out of their conflict.)

As the consultation drew to an end, I elicited
reactions to the session and pointed to further direc-
ions, yet Fred and Leslie did not let go of their father. Obviously, they wanted to get more mileage out
of the consultation ... (By this time little Mary had
gone back to her mother). I intervened strongly and
pointed out that the young people apparently wanted to
make up for lost time in the past. But I was worried
about Harry who, after taking a tremendous step by
agreeing to do something as difficult for him as the
visit to the cemetery, would now be asked to do too
many things at once. He then would probably revert to
his old pattern and the family would once again be
where they started. While saying this, the consultant
changed seats with Leslie and moved close to Harry,
directing her words intently to him. He confirmed
that he felt "numb" from all the pressures. "Go slow,
one thing at a time" was the message the consultant
gave the family. Yet, at the very last moment and almost missed by the consultant, Florence took the half-
asleep Mary, handed her to Harry who picked her up,
and carried her out of the room! This is how the family looked in the closing moments of the session:

Diagram IV

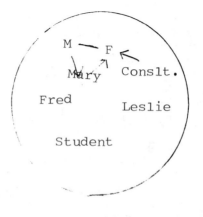

98

4. AFTER THE CONSULTATION

There was a lot of emotion expressed immediately after the family departed. Notably, empathy regarding the father. A few students recognized that their feelings had shifted from anger (passivity is always something which angers people) to almost tender feelings toward him. Surprise was expressed about Fred, who did not look "sociopathic" to anybody. Many students quite rightfully were worried about the marriage.

When the class met again one week later, most students were able to draw the picture of the family very accurately. Nevertheless, a few missed some points and did not always see the connections. They were amazed that the pre-discussion had been on target in some, but not in other ways; e.g., the assumed natural father-children coalition had not been borne out. The class was able to acknowledge the important work that their colleague had done in earlier sessions. They were pleased to learn that the father had subsequently taken the children to the cemetery. In addition to the points made in the description of the interview itself, I, as the instructor, dealt with the danger of expecting "too much". We discussed possible strategy as to how to deal with this, We speculated that the marital relationship would become more focal, and that Fred may well bail the parents out by means of acting out, thus reverting to his accustomed role. It is sometimes useful to predict to a family what may happen, thus lessening the likelihood of its occurrence. Re-enforcement of the sibling and the parental-marital system as well as the necessity of dealing with as yet uncovered areas, i.e., "Paul and the family" (with the possibility of inviting Paul to come to a family session) and some exploration regarding the dead mother and her relatives were added to the strategic armamentarium of the student worker.

The question of reassessing family members by seeing them within the context of the family always comes up. Therefore, I asked the students how they saw Fred, especially in view of the bleak psychological test and his molestation of Mary, the incident which brought him to the attention of the protective agency. The students marveled at the quantity and quality of his participation and how "un-sociopathic"

he had seemed, particularly when his behavior was
viewed in the light and the context of a certain situation and within family transactions "then and now".
I had to push a little about the behavior between
brother and half-sister; the students were aware
that there was no visible transaction between them.
This fact could be construed as both suspicious or reassuring. I pointed out, however, that I had watched
carefully whether Mary had looked at her brother either in a coquettish or in a frightened way. There
was no evidence of either, not even body tension.
Neither did the family directly or indirectly refer
to the incident. All of this made me believe that we
were dealing with an isolated incident. Some students
recalled that at one point I quite deliberately, albeit in a casual manner, mentioned the subject. This
was done in line with my belief that any pssible taboo area needs to be "untabooed". Therefore, when
Fred moved his chair close to his stepmother and
acted somewhat seductively to which she reacted
pleasurably, I commented that since in their family
everybody was so hungry for love and nobody knew how
to get it, the lines occasiohally got mixed up. In
the discussion I elaborated upon this, speculating
that Fred, the well-developed adolescent, unquestion-
ably was drawn to his attractive stepmother, especially since he was only too aware of the sexual
coolness between his father and her (in the marital
discussion the issue of Harry wanting more sex and
Florence more help, and tenderness, came out). Moreover, with Fred's impulse control not fully devehoped,
yet conscious of the existing incest taboo regarding
even a not blood related parent, it may have needed
merely one unguarded moment, possibly when Fred was
angry with his stepmother, for such an incident to
take place. There was agreement that working with
one individual in this family or only the marital
pair would miss the core transactions and in all likelihood, not alter the system.

5. RELUCTANCE TO USE LIVE FAMILIES

There are various reasons why an instructor may
hesitate to function in the role of consultant in a
demonstration interview. Aside from the possible
lack of expertise as a clinician or the somewhat slow
and awesome process necessary to get the students to
cooperate in providing a live family, the element of
unpredictability is probably the greatest single fac-

tor in making an instructor in the academic setting
shy away from this productive teaching tool. Unpredictability can occur in a variety of ways. It can
range from the family that simply does not show up
for the consultation (although this is unusual) to unexpected events which arise from within the interview
and which create the type of crisis that can be disconcerting to the consultant-teacher, or the students,
or the family. For me personally, the worst that can
happen is not being able to find entrance to the family system. This would be rare, but it is always a
possibility. We are talking about the kind of family
that will organize itself to defeat the consultant.
The reasons for it are not easily determined: they
may be related to the lack of preparation, or the
quality of relationship the regular therapist has
with the family. They may lie in the situation itself, or, of course, in the intangible area between
the consultant and the family that may lead the consultant to make the wrong therapeutic moves.

An example of this blocking out of the therapist
is the following: a black, divorced woman with three
children, two girls 14 and 12, and a boy 8, were
brought to class by a student who had worked with the
mother individually. The woman, Mrs. L, had been divorced for many years. Her husband lived out of
state and had kept erratic contact with his children.
Her oldest son, a boy of 15, not brought to the session, had given her trouble ever since the father's
departure (or to be more precise - was kicked out by
the mother). A few months preceding the session, the
boy had been placed in a home for disturbed children
due to his severely acting-out behavior that extended to the community and school and was, of course manifest in the home. He did not adjust to the insti-
tution, in part because the mother had allegedly sa-
botaged the plan, and, in part, because his father
had sent out signals "inviting the boy to live with
him and his mother" (the boy's grandmother). The boy,
Johnny, ran away to his father. Whereupon the exas-
perated child-care worker, who did not really like
Mrs. L, arranged for Johnny to stay in his father's
home, after a merely superficial investigation and
without consulting Mrs. L (sic!). This was done in
spite of the fact that the mother was the boy's legal
guardian. Mrs. L, understandably, was infuriated and
turned to the agency with which she had had past con-
tact(mostly providing her with tangible services), and
was assigned to our student. It became quickly ap-

101

parent to the student that there was a lot of trouble in the household beyond the actual crisis, some of it between the mother and her youngest son who was destined to follow in his brother's footsteps. Mrs. L agreed to bring her family to the class consultation.

On the basis of the pre-consultation discussion we decided to focus not only on the actual crisis but to test whether the family could deal with the issue of the loss of the father (the divorce) and the loss of the oldest brother. We also planned to give attention to the complaints about the youngest son Michael, and the shy and withdrawn behavior of the girls. We agreed to explore whether Mrs. L could be persuaded to collaborate with her former husband to plan for Johnny. It was agreed that all agencies involved with the family needed to be included in the planning. Throughout the discussion the student gave no clue that the woman was disturbed.

In the actual session, Mrs. L, a handsome, well-educated woman, a nurse by profession, used every opportunity to impress her status upon the consultant and the group. She also managed to defeat every effort that I made to establish rapport, or to work on any area that she was supposedly concerned about. Nor did she allow me to "touch" any of her children. This was in spite of Michael's somewhat irrepressible efforts to give away some "secrets", namely that he was missing his father and brother, had trouble in school and at home, etc. Each statement he made was invalidated by the mother while the girls looked petrified. Similarly, she rejected any attempt I made to discuss the situation about her son, Johnny, despite my full recognition that Mrs. L had good reason to be angry with both the child care agency and her former husband. It was particularly disconcerting to me, the consultant, when Mrs. L denied having had any difficulty with Johnny whereupon she introduced in a casual way certain dramatic things: for example, that she was suffering from cancer, while a few moments later when I tried to explore this with her, she announced that she was planning to adopt a child. Rational and irrational statements were intermingled, and although the superficial impression was one of logical rationality, contradictions were manifest. When I introduced the racial issue as a possible reason for her fighting everything I said, Mrs. L responded in the affirmative, insisting that "nobody was on her side", except perhaps the student, who in-

102

cidentally was white. Yet, simultaneously she insisted that she liked the consultant and the consultation itself. In despair, I finally turned to the group and asked them to help us with the impass. The students made every effort to reach Mrs. L; one black student shared her own experiences in a hostile world, a divorced mother spoke about her own feelings of being trapped and often helpless with regard to her adolescent children, yet nothing appeared to make any difference, Mrs. L responded in the same way to challenging as well as supportive statements. When I decided to terminate the interview Mrs. L insisted on staying on, and forced me into an authoritative role. The student reported that when she drove the family home the mother spoke of how "nice it had been" and then did not further refer to the consultation.

In our post-demonstration class discussion there was a considerable amount of speculation about the meaning of this. (There was also some relief expressed that there were situations in which even an experienced clinician could fail!) Without going into the details we conjectured about the elements that possibly led to the failure:

1) The woman was obviously disturbed and I had been quite unprepared for this
2) Mrs. L had not expected a "treatment interview" at all, since her idea of help had been that of tangible services
3) She must have perceived the "invasion" of the system by a stranger as terribly threatening but because of her denial pattern could only deal with it in a totally irrational way; thus, the consultant, like so many other people, became the "enemy" who had to be defeated. In one way, I had been drawn into the system and when my efforts did not pay off, I, as do others in desparation, tried "more of the same", instead of changing my strategy. It probably would have been more helpful if I had interrupted the interview earlier, sent the family out and engaged in a discussion with the group about strategy, e.g., putting the woman in a paradoxical situation, by advising her that she was correct and nobody could help her with so knotty a problem, etc.

Nonetheless, the discussion gave the students a

103

fuller picture of the woman's and the system's disturbance. It also allowed us to think of ways in
which we could work with the other agency, rather
than changing the family, as well as the father and
grandmother, and only involve Mrs. L in plans in relation to her wayward son, (something which she after
all had requested). From what I heard last, the student reported that a visit between the father, son,
and the family had taken place though nothing more
permanent had been worked out.

Acting out is another type of unpredictability.
Here are two illustrations[3] showing how "acting out"
in the session, if appropriately handled, can lead to
a meaningful and productive interview. The first example is of a family which perceived the group as dangerous. This was the B family, whose 11-year old
daughter, Jeanie, suffered from school phobia. The
worker had prepared the family for the demonstration
interview and they had agreed to it. Nevertheless,
when the family walked toward the interviewing room
the child became so agitated that neither her parents
nor the worker could persuade the child to enter.
The class and instructor heard the commotion, which
went on for quite some time. The students expected
the instructor to figure out a way to get the entire
family into the classroom, yet the instructor was not
sure of how to do this. Only when she verbalized her
feelings and "permitted a way out" (namely to interview the family if need be in privacy), did she re-
gain her self-assuredness. She joined the family in
the corridor and began talking to the parents about
the panic which the child had expressed, and about
their helplessness. She responded especially to the
parents' "fear" of the child, which they expressed
through alternating threats, cajolery, and promises,
all of which only bewildered Jeanie more. The instructor then suggested that it was quite all right
if the family came to the room without Jeanie, per-
mitting her to join the others "if and when she felt
ready". While it was apparent that the parents too
were frightened and by now also ashamed (in fact,
they later turned out to be as phobic as the child)
they finally entered the room with the siblings following them. The interview was most productive. Jeanie first stood by the door, which the instructor had
left open, and finally - when she became convinced
that nothing dreadful was happening, sat down on the
chair that had been invitingly placed for her near
the door.

104

A second case of unpredictable acting-out was
that of Mr. G who had just come out of jail. Mrs. G
acted the part of the martyr, and had successfully
convinced her four children that she had no choice
but to leave their father because he was "no good",
not a bit interested in them and totally unreliable.
The father had begged for another chance with his family and while not willing to be "in treatment" had
agreed to come to the family consultation. In the
course of the session it became clear that not all the
children were "anti-father" and that the mother was
in part using them against him. When the consultant
consistently stopped her "slugging" him, she finally
began to talk about her feelings of loneliness due to
his having "deserted" her and not really ever having
met her needs. Tears ran down the cheeks of this
otherwise cool, judgmental woman. At that moment the
husband (a powerful, six-foot black man who, throughout the session had been extremely ill at ease and defensive) shouted something and stormed out of the
room. The instructor immediately followed him, acting upon her belief that any acting-out in a session
should be dealt with right away. Nonetheless, the instructor was a bit frightened. But when she got to
the hallway, she saw the man had placed himself opposite the exit, in an almost totally trapped position, instead of running out into the street. The instructor walked close to him and gently touched his
arm, speaking quietly. She expressed her feelings
that something must have made him terribly angry and
upset in the session. He glared at her as she continued talking, mentioning as possible reasons the
racial factor, the exposure by his wife and the feeling that the class might have pre-judged him. Slowly
his tense muscles softened; he bellowed that he was
not angry but could not stand his wife's tears because they made him feel soft. He agreed to come
back into the room, giving the instructor permission
to tell his family why he had run out. When they returned, it was obvious that his wife had used his
exodus to justify her wrath against him, getting the
children and the observing group on her side. It was
quite a revelation to everyone, when the instructor
shared with them the real reason for Mr. G's running
out of the room. This, together with the subsequent
discussion began to correct the one-sided image the
family and the therapist had had of him.

Sometimes the whole family may not appear. Naturally, in such a case, the students are disappointed,

and the student who had made the family arrangements
is dismayed. He will even most likely apologize as
if, indeed, it had been his failure! Not unlike the
Parental Child who carries more responsibility than
the others, he will assume more than his share. This
gives the instructor the opportunity to focus on the
group transactions in relation to disappointments and
stimulate their problem solving abilities. Thus in
such a contingency I use role playing. The students
can substitute for the family in line with the previous strategy or they can focus on the next session.

Sometimes, unpredictably, only a sub-group shows
up. In one class that I conducted, we had planned
for a two-generational session with a couple locked
in marital difficulties, not being able to make progress. The instructor had suggested in planning to
get the couple to bring the man's parents to the consultation. The man had agreed. The choice of asking
his parents was made in view of the student's assessment that the young man's fear of his father played
an important role in the marital difficulty.

On the day of the consultation the student-worker
was informed that the couple would be coming alone.
In a quick pre-session discussion, I asked the students whether they would be ready to stand in for the
parents if and when I thought this would be useful.
The students agreed and the interview began. After a
short period the wife loudly proclaimed her contempt
for her weak husband. I then suggested that the husband choose a set of parents from among the students
and instruct them as to how they should behave. Somewhat shyly, the young man got up and after some
searching selected two students (one male and one female). He described his father as powerful, always
critical and his mother as nice, but helpless. Upon
being asked when he had begun to see these characteristics in his parents, he recalled a childhood scene
that he was then asked to play out.

Tommy (the man) was a fearful child and his father was determined to make him brave and manly.
Once when he was approximately 9 years old, he was
asked to go to a neighborhood store to get a news paper. This meant that he had to pass the house of a
neighbor who had a somewhat fierce dog, of which Tommy was afraid. Urged by his father to show that he
was a "man" the boy proceeded to go. However, unbeknownst to him the father followed and unleashed the

dog who not only barked, but jumped on the boy when he passed. Tommy was petrified and in a panic threw himself to the ground while the dog, probably harmless, hovered over him, barking. The scene ended with the father rescuing the boy and the mother taking the sobbing child into her arms.

The students and I watched the scene with horror. I noticed too that the young wife had been crying silently. In the remainder of the session she was soft and gentle to her husband, while he, in a more self-assertive way enumerated the things he did not like in her.

Thus, there are many ways in which unexpected, unpredictable events in the classroom demonstration can be utilized to add to the students' experience and to enhance the level of skill.

The value of the demonstration interview lies in the first-hand experience the students have with seeing how a family interview can be handled. It allows for maximum engagement through planning, experiencing and thinking through without the student doing the job himself. It allows the student to learn through observation and participation, through being both part of and outside the system. It gives the student-therapist a chance to see how his family engages with another therapist and to learn through watching a model. The family in turn has a chance to be exposed to an expert in the protective presence of their therapist while at the same time being exposed to the "world". Without minimizing the elements of anxiety due to this, the anonymous observing group is often experienced by the family as reflecting society and as being interested in their plight. "I never knew that so many people cared" said one family member after a consultation. Whatever the family's perception and reaction to being observed might be, the consultant and the student-trainee's use of the setting and the dynamics inherent in it are important. If universities have a one-way mirror, the family can be given the opportunity to choose between the illusion of being protected (they are being seen without seeing) or to deal with the open observation. It should be noted that many families when given the opportunity have opted for the open setting.

REFERENCES

1. Napier, A.Y., "The Consultation-Demonstration Interview" in _Family Process_, December 1976.

2. Schulman, G.L., "Myths that Intrude on the Adaptation of the Stepfamily" in _Social Casework_, March 1972.

3. _____, "Teaching Family Therapy to Social Work Students" in _Social Casework_, July 1976.

CHAPTER VII

TEACHING AND TREATMENT TECHNIQUES

The therapist or educator can employ a variety of
techniques, depending upon the particular purpose he
has in mind. Unfortunately, some therapists become
enamored or critical, as the case may be, of a given
technique, using it indiscriminately or rejecting it
in toto. Neither is desirable. Nevertheless, depending upon the orientation of the therapist, he will be
inclined to utilize certain techniques while rejecting others.

For instance, structurally* oriented family therapists find the giving of tasks most useful, whereas
psychodynamically oriented family therapists like to
use imagery, fantasy or even dream material. The
strategic[1] school often gives "prescriptions" in the
form of carefully worded letters which are either
handed to the family at the end of a session or sent
by mail. Sometimes instructions in the form of certain rituals accompany the prescriptions: like who,
when, and how a letter should be read. Certain techniques may be particularly useful for training purposes while others may be better for the direct use
with families. In my opinion, a technique such as
Bowen's coaching** is specifically designed to help

---

*Notably Dr. S. Minuchin and Jay Haley

**Coaching is a technique which is aimed at influenc-
ing the family system through working with one or two
key people in their family. An example of this would
be an adult daughter, overclose and too dependent on
her mother and too distant from her father. The
therapist would suggest that in her daily telephone
call to her mother, some of it devoted to complaints
about the father, daughter requests to speak to her
father about something of interest to him. If this

individuals influence the family system, if the family is not available or if the therapist deems their presence unnecessary. (It is also an excellent training tool that enables therapists to work with their own families without bringing them directly into treatment).

Techniques aim at broadening the treatment base through new cognitive or emotional understanding. They also enable the family and its members to find alternate ways of behaving and to try out this new behavior. The goal of any technique is change, whether the change occurs within a person through the broadening of some perspective, the replacement of old sterotypical thinking or through new behavior. Techniques prvide individuals and families with new options and, therefore, with new aspects of reality, thus being essentially growth-producing. Without in any way aiming at being all-inclusive, those techniques that are most commonly employed in the field of family therapy for both training and treatment purposes will be discussed, including two of the most popular techniques - role playing and sculpting. These are borrowed from the creative arts (the drama) and the representative arts (drawing and sculpting) and aim at providing a bridge to real life. Through their partial detouring of language which is linear, they emphasize the circulatory aspect of transactions which may lead to new options.

Role Playing

This technique aims at approximating life, so that the "hearsay" and the "talked about" which are at best thin replicas of reality, can be experienced more directly and immediately. It aims at recreating the emotional climate of an event with a view toward ex-

---

(ctd. from precedimg page)

is done, the mother may feel hurt and complain to father about the daughter, something which may lead to solidification of the parental axis against the daughter, thus freeing her from the enmeshment with the other generation; or it could at least balance the mother-daughter bond through giving father some direct access to the daughter.

panding the narrow subjective confines of what may be
reported in a casual and subjective manner. (The
originator of this technique, on which many others
are based, is Moreno, the founder of Psycho-drama.
His influence is still widely felt). Because of the
emotional element of these mini-dramas they are particularly useful in evoking hidden and repressed emotions both in relation to events of the distant or immediate past and the everyday life of the family. Beyond the emotional impact they also provide the on-
looker (therapist-teacher) with material that is rarely forthcoming through verbal accounts. There are dimensions which are not readily available to the subject, wuch as multiple non-verbal transactions conveyed by means of body gestures and positions and
metaphors existing in human behavior. Videotapes
have been extremely helpful in connection with this
technique. They show family members how they act
with each other since most people are not or are only
dimly aware of the quality and even the occurrence of
their non-verbal communications. They rarely know
the impact these communications have on other people,
especially if they are repetitive. The "finger point-
ing 'blamer'"[2] or the "eyebrow lifting" criticizer is
amazed to see how people react to "so innocent a gesture". The same person may also, once aware of the
gesture, decide to "get rid of it".

Role playing also allows for a broader view of
transactions, one that is less related to cause and
blame than to the multiplicity and circularity of human transactions. For example, the older sibling who
is being punished for beating up the younger child
may be more sympathetically treated by the parents in
the re-creation of the incident when they witness the
younger child's pestering of the older one and his
not responding to milder forms of reprimand. This
kind of "play out" also allows for on the spot intervention, i.e., "corrective actions". Thus, fuller
knowledge of an incident may lead to new ways of dealing with a situation. Parents may be helped to stay
out of sibling fights or at least not ally themselves
with one or another child against the other offspring.

The playing out of scenes is helpful with families
that are poor informants of events which may lead to
inaccurate premises* on the part of the therapist.

---

* (see following page)

In regard to other families, especially those that need to present themselves as being "without flaw" or those that are given to intellectualization or verbosity, an action-play oriented technique has obvious advantages. Sometimes it is difficult for the therapist to get a picture of the position of certain family members and their relationship to each other. Who has not heard the monosyllabic "father is o.k." or "grandpa is not interested" or "mother is on the 'phone". The feelings of the person making these statements is rather evident; less clear, however, are the circumstances under which such behavior occurs and who the less obvious participants are and what solution can be found if the behavior is dysfunctional.

In all these, as well as other instances, I like to introduce the playing out of ordinary but crucial everyday life occurrences such as "when father comes home from work" or "family dinner", "bedtime" or "waking up time", etc. The person who directs the "playlet" is told to position the family members in the way that they normally are positioned just before "Dad comes home"; they have to be directed to sit in a certain way, smile or be serious and to look in a particular direction.

In one such scene the "sassy" problem child, a boy of 10, positioned his mother who had never mentioned any dissatisfaction with her husband, in the kitchen. She was busily preparing dinner while trying to ward off the attention-demanding 5-year old daughter. The boy noisily ran in and out of the kitchen, indicating that he was starving. When the father entered the door, there was a moment of expectant silence and the wife turned to him with a smile. The father went to the refrigerator, took a drink, patted the wife on the back and went to the bathroom

---

* (from preceding page)
In a book edited by Peggy Papp, Family Therapy, Full Length Case Studies, Gardner Press, Inc. 1977, p.198 M. Walters gives an example of an event that the family never clarified. While the author minimizes the importance of it, it is in my opinion obvious that there are situations in which it is essential to get facts due to legal or safety components.

to wash up. At this point the mother pushed her little daughter out of the way and scolded her 10-year old son who had also first glanced at his father. It is important in the debriefing phase for the therapist not to identify with one member of the family against another, nor to leave anybody out of the discussion. The father was asked what he expected prior to entering the house. He replied that he had hoped that dinner would be ready and on the table or that his wife would meet him at the door, inquiring how his day had been at the office. When this did not happen, he withdrew, mildly disappointed, into the bathroom. This mild disappointment changed to outright annoyance when he heard the commotion in the kitchen. As happened in this case, family members are often astonished to hear each other's verbalization of wishes, hopes and disappointments, as well as the imputed meaning given to each other's actions. There are no villains in this everyday family, just mini-crises that may or may not maintain the system, the symptom of which may be the troubled boy.

Role playing is by far the most popular tool used in teaching and training. It is particularly helpful in demonstrating to students how it feels to be in certain positions or to carry certain roles. For instance, the instructor may suggest that the student position himself outside the family circle while the rest of the family is huddled together. Within a short time the student will experience the kind of feelings that are generally associated with being an "outcast" and "alone". Allow the "family" to whisper something inaudible and the same student will begin to feel "suspect", "talked about" and eventually, angry. Hence, psychiatric labels such as "paranoid" or "depressed" can take on an interactional rather than an intra-psychic meaning.

Interviews can be role played as well. In this way the student can not only get a sense of what it is like to be a family member but how to operate as a family therapist. Initially the instructor may need to function as a temporary "alter ego" of the student-therapist, but later in the semester other students may take over when the role-playing student-therapist feels stuck or appears to wander too far afield.

In one of my classes, a great deal of skepticism regarding initial family sessions was expressed. I suggested that the student most doubtful about the process "interview" the "mother" who had requested help out of concern for her child. It became a typical not even imaginative "talk session" in which a great deal of information was accumulated which led to nowhere. Suddenly the student said to the mother, "I can't make head or tail of what you tell me; next time I will need to see your entire family". She then picked up "a family" of two "parents" and two "children" from the class and interviewed them. In the process she picked up on such phenomena as parental sabotaging, favoritism of one child and a weak sibling sub-system. She terminated the interview asking the family to return "next week" for more exploration.

Like any other group, a student group is a "natural" for role playing since the student plays a simulated part. In a family session, the individual member has to either be himself or play another family member. The latter is particularly helpful if a person finds herself unable to change or to empathize with another family member. Such exercises lead to greater identification and empathy. If a family is not complete, gestalt exercises can be very helpful. Most frequently used are devices like "talking to an empty chair" in an imaginary dialogue with a dead or feared parent. This can enable a person (with impunity) to say "forbidden" things to his parent to which the "parent" can then respond. The role of the imaginary parent can either be carried by the therapist or by the person himself. Role playing is a rehearsal which may lead to actions in real life, although they may remain within the confines of the therapeutic situation. Nevertheless, they tend to clarify a person's feelings, including the response of another, all of which, albeit in a less direct way, can lead to change.

Sculpting

In contrast to the above described technique in which events are played out close to the actual life situation and which aim at maximizing the emotional impact inherent in a situation, the technique of sculpting[3] or spatialization aims at the opposite: namely, at the distancing of oneself from the highly emotional component inherent in one's own family. In contrast to role playing, speaking is discouraged. The "sculptor" positions his family in the way he envisions them in his own mind, mapping out certain as-

pects of the relationship such as distance and power.
He adds to the tool of sculpting the "paintbrush"
with which he puts facial expressions on his objects.
Therefore, the picture of the "artist's" internal reality emerges, which makes various components visible
and accessible to his and other people's study. When
finished the sculptor can step back and change his
work until he is ultimately satisfied. Thus, he looks
at his own creation (vision) more like an outsider,
an objective observer. As the "observing ego" is
freed in the process, the artist is able to disengage
himself and look at the complex relational composition
in new ways. The sculptor can also use another person
as a stand-in for himself. Fine touches can always
be added: some may involve movement such as when a
person is asked to first look into one and then another direction, much as a mechanical doll would. It
is an intricate and paradoxical process through which
a person will create himself in his family group while
at the same time remaining outside of it (similar to
a self-portrait by a painter). Metaphors used in
language confirm the concept of spatial and visual
analogies as when we talk about the "landscape of the
mind", "bridging the gap", "climbing a mountain" or
"getting our feet wet", or when we refer to "emotional distance".

The people in the sculpture can either remain motionless (and if so should be allowed to stand for a
few minutes so that the impact of the sculpting can
impress itself upon one's mind) or, as already indicated, can engage in some brief body movements. These
movements usually reflect either indecision on the
part of the sculptor or two different positions on
the part of an object. For instance, a child pulled
between his two parents or one who is the "go-between"
in the family. It is thus important that the therapist or teacher remain sensitive to clues and introduce additional or modifying techniques to allow for
a fuller transposition of the subject's reality.

Once, in working with a couple, the author was
unable to get them to stop their repetitive description of the wife's dominance and the husband's sub-
mission. When I asked the wife to sculpt her relationship with her husband she put him, much to my
amazement, on a high chair in the position of a
"grand seigneur" or "savior". She looked at him with
an admiring gaze. Later, she made him come down from
his pedestal, after which both talked to each other

as peers would.

In an extremely sensitive videotape, "Making the Invisible Visible"*, Peggy Papp combines the work of all family members in one exercise. She begins with one person who does the sculpting for a while until another person indicates that he can add something to the picture at which point she lets this person take over. Thus, she moves from one to another and allows a dynamic picture to emerge composed by all family members. She calls this technique, accurately, "family choreography". This process adds richly to the original dimension of sculpting and stimulates the therapist to draw upon his own creativity as an artist and healer.

Most novice therapists (students) worry about the initial steps necessary to get a sculpting going and fear being laughed at by the family (a resistance in which the student-therapist readily joins in, since he too is unaccustomed to use body and metaphorical language). It is true that most families need some help to engage in the process. Yet, the TV generation of today catches on easily and even loves the opportunity to operate as stage directors. If the technique is used in class, educators (or therapists) need to actively help the "would be sculptor" by showing him what to do initially and then continue to "give him a hand" in the process. A joke such as "I am not expecting an Oscar performance" sometimes breaks the ice.

The question as to who should be the sculptor often arises among students. As do most of the decisions of this sort in a treatment situation, the choice depends on many factors. Personally, I often begin with the person who is most likely to enjoy the sculpting and of course preference is given to the "volunteer". The problem carrier is avoided in line with my tendency to avoid focusing on the scapegoat or patient, since he is most likely to be the one interfered with by the family. In general, I prefer to have at least two people in a family engage in sculpting since one of the messages conveyed to the family

---

*This videotape can be rented from the Ackerman Family Institute

through this technique is the unique inimitable way in which things can be viewed. Furthermore, that differences are not related to "right or wrong" but to the internal perception people bring to a situation, that, among other things, is determined by the position a person has in the family. (I often refer to this phenomenon as the Rashomon syndrome from the Japanese film "Rashomon", in which at least four different versions of the same event are portrayed).

Sometimes sculpting is a good method to pull in a silent member of the family. In one family an "obstinate" adolescent participated for the first time in a family session announcing in advance that she would not talk. The therapist, in an attempt to avoid a struggle with the youngster, asked the mother to sculpt the family as if she would be "Annie", The mother obliged, only to be interrupted by the teenager who corrected her! In this way the adolescent did exactly what the therapist had hoped she would do, namely give her picture of the family.

Though the experience of the actual sculpting carries considerable power in and of itself, most experts agree that the process of discussing the experience, the debriefing, is most important so that people can draw conclusions from it. The family members are asked to share their feelings and observations. Often a lively dialogue ensues in which things get revealed and family members get a better sense as to how the rest of the family perceives a situation in which they are all involved. The family also can move toward arranging the family in a more suitable way. Thus, solutions are sometimes found by the family itself without much verbal interchange.

If sculpting or the playing out of a family scene is being used as a teaching instrument, the observers are first asked to describe what they perceived, especially in relation to sequential transactions. More than anything else, this allows the students to conceptualize the development of sequences and to see the roles "innocent bystanders" sometimes play in what may be presented as a dyadic transaction.

It takes some doing to enable the actual "players" of the scene (or the figures of a sculpture) to wait for the sharing of their experiences, as there is considerable pressure built up during the exercise. However, as a teacher I give priority to the sharpen-

ing of the students' observational ability, which
would be unwittingly contaminated by the precipitous
sharing of the experience by those who played the
roles.

A word of caution to those students who leave a
family at the end of a sculpting session with the
idealized picture of their "wished for reality". In
too many family sculptings, even those done by the
most rebellious adolescent, the wished for family is
depicted as standing close to each other in a circle,
members holding on to each other and turned inward.
Since this idealized picture is often shared by the
therapist, who may be tired of the frequent struggles
and alienation occurring in most families in treatment, he joins the system. The result is that the
family will be bitterly disappointed when, upon their
return to reality, the old patterns of behavior re-
emerge. In my opinion, it is essential to "burst the
bubble" before an explosion occurs. Similar to the
therapist who warns a family that has made progress
"not to go so fast", the therapist after a sculpting
session needs to help the family move back to reality.
Beyond this, however, the idealized "togetherness" is
often not at all appropriate in terms of the developmental stage the family is in. In such a case, the
family as well as the adolescent has to let go rather
than cling and be enmeshed. A casual comment like:
"you would feel pretty choked if you would have to
stay this way all the time" or "how would Dad go to
work and junior to his baseball game" may evoke some
laughter and break the "charm of the circle". The
therapist has to introduce the difference between wish
and reality and speak about the importance of growth
as well as distance and separateness in order to, at
other times, appreciate closeness and intimacy. Moreover, the difference between an adolescent and the
married couple has to be emphasized.

Tasks

Somewhat frowned upon as simplistic and too direc-
tive by some more traditional therapists, tasks are
excellent techniques for introducing change in a system. While certain tasks appear to be simple, the
planning of a task, especially one which involves the
whole system, is really quite complex in nature. Certain tasks are natural results of a given session like
the proposed visit to the cemetery by the P family,

discussed in Chapter VI. Other tasks are organiza-
tional in nature, like the distribution of household
chores. Still others enable a family to do things
that they have never done before, such as when in a
child-centered family the marital pair is encouraged
to go out on their own during the weekend. While simple and direct the execution of such a task necessi-
tates a great deal of preparation. Firstly, the
couple has to have reached some stage of readiness to
be on their own and the family, if there are young
children, must be able to utilize other systems, siblings or grandparents, etc. so that the plan can become operational. Also it may force the family to
deal with issues they may have avoided. A couple
might hide their marital problems behind the "uncooperative" behavior of their children and the children,
being part of the system, may help their parents avoid
whatever the painful issues may be. Tasks sometimes
help to explode the myth (the myth being that the
couple cannot be on their own due to their children's
misbehavior) and the couple has no choice but to deal
with the marital situation.

As already indicated strategic family therapists
often use complicated paradoxical prescriptions which
may involve tasks. However, the way these prescriptions or tasks are transmitted add another dimension
to the effectiveness of the treatment process. This
is in part related to the structure in which the interview takes place. The interviewing therapist is
a member of a treatment team which is placed - known
to the family - behind a one-way mirror; the team
intervenes from time to time according to their assessment of the process. The team either calls the
interviewing therapist out or the therapist leaves on
his own and joins the group. Together they discuss
the appropriate strategy. Much like a messenger he
then returns to the family and informs them of the
"recommendations" of the anonymous group; recommendations he may or may not "agree"with or "differ"
from. The split approach puts the family into a paradoxical situation, in which hope and doubt are expressed simultaneously. This type of therapy does
not favor involving the family in a treatment plan
by letting them directly participate, nor does it
value awareness or "open communication" or "expres-
sive feelings". Instead, the therapeutic team tries
to define the core problem and its unconscious-irra-
tional component within the family system on which
they base their strategy. This may consist in "pre-

scribing the symptom within the system" or any other
paradoxical intervention.

In my opinion this approach is too complicated to
teach to a beginning family therapist unless he is
placed in an agency in which he would be part of an
experienced team. However, some of the basic concepts
underlying this approach are part of my teaching.

Thus, different from giving advice, straight or
paradoxical tasks always take the entire system into
consideration. Moreover, the follow-up of the tasks
is an essential part of the process. Students are
therefore taught to inquire what happens to a given
task, even if the family does not refer to it. The
tracking of the process provides the student-worker
with crucial material related to such questions as
"how far the task has progressed", "who was responsible for the breakdown, when and under what circumstances did it occur". Depending on the class, a new
assessment can be made which either leads to a repetition or a modification of the task, or to a replacement of it by a different one (which may be not to
give a task at all); sometimes families come up with
some suggestions on their own.

Charting

The visualization of a system offers students,
who by and large are acculturated to relate by way of
words, a new way of conveying to themselves and others
what a system looks like, especially in structural
terms. The charting or drawing of a family is an excellent teaching tool. It shortens the often cumber-
some process of telling innumerable details that add
little to the basic understanding of the family.
Charting forces the student to look at a family in a
special way. Two principal ways in which a family
diagram can be drawn are:

1. The Genogram*

The genogram is a family tree that shows the development of a family over at least three generations.
Its aim is to show how patterns are transmitted and
how past events such as death, illness, etc. have in-

---

*Developed by Dr. Murray Bowen and his school

fluenced current patterns and how they affect family
dyads and triangles. It allows both the therapist and
the family to view these phenomena together. At times
it brings "skeletons out of the closet" and in general
it permits a rich vertical view of the family. This
approach has some similarity to the more traditional
history-taking approach, except that it is pattern-
and structure-oriented and it is done through charting rather than verbally. In most cases it involves
the family in the process.

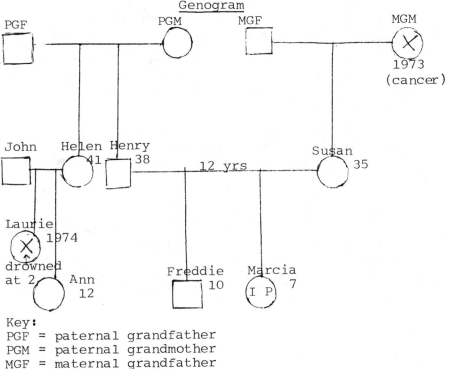

Genogram

Key:
PGF = paternal grandfather
PGM = paternal grandmother
MGF = maternal grandfather
MGM = maternal grandmother

Henry and Susan applied to the agency because of
Marcia's timidity and fear of peers. Two cogent
events appearing on the genogram may have influenced
H's and S's attitude in relation to Marcia. Susan's
mother died shortly before Marcia's birth, the same
year Helen's 2-year old daughter drowned. These trig-
ger events may not immediately be known to a therapist
who, like the author, approaches families first in relation to their current nuclear structure, although he

121

would, of course, inquire re the impacting systems (grandparents, adult siblings, etc.) and would pick up the theme of anxiety in the family which eventually would lead to above information.

2. Family Constellation Charts (Eco-Charts)

The author prefers to begin with a schematic drawing of the family system, as it appears at present, especially for teaching purposes. Similar to family sculpture, it emphasizes the boundaries around a family and within the family. These include the generational lines, the hierarchical and spatial positions and indications of positive, negative and loose relationships. Since a family system is not only seen as an isolated unit but is influenced by other systems (the importance of which varies) the diagram is expanded to include these other systems in relation to their significance to the target unit.

Nevertheless, in line with the author's thinking, it does not ignore the importance of past events.* However, these events are regarded in terms of changes within the family constellation, that, as was previously discussed, are seen as profoundly influential not only to family structure (position and alliances) but also to feelings and attitudes or patterns resulting from them. For example, the student who discusses a family is asked to "help me", i.e., the instructor to put the current family configuration on the blackboard. He is also requested to draw (or help me to draw) those systems which seem to influence the current family situation:

---

* Family event charts and the genogram itself are also used, but not as a primary tool

122

Family Constellation Chart

(Family as it appears at present)

3 years

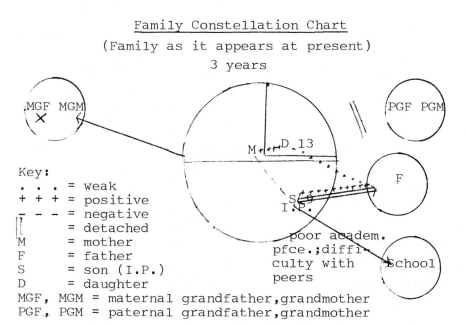

Key:
. . . = weak
+ + + = positive
- - - = negative
⎸⎹ = detached
M = mother
F = father
S = son (I.P.)
D = daughter
MGF, MGM = maternal grandfather,grandmother
PGF, PGM = paternal grandfather,grandmother

The preceding diagram shows a single parent family of
three years' duration. The oldest child, a daughter,
is the parental child and the youngest son is strongly
connected with the father. The fact that the drawing
includes the school, with which the boy is negatively
connected, indicates that there is some trouble in
this system. It can be noted that the two events,
the boy's starting school and the father's leaving
the house occurred at the same time. The inclusion
of the school and the divorced father reminds the student that in the process of working with the family,
neither the father nor the school should be ignored.
Many family therapists who work toward improvement of
family relationships, neglect other important systems
such as the school[5] that may contribute in its own
way or sustain some of the difficulties.

Next, the student-worker is asked to draw what
the family may have looked like at the point when the
current constellation (structure) had first changed;
in this case, just prior to the father's leaving the
family. Though this chart is hypothetical, there are
clues in the current constellation that indicate what
may have been. It stimulates the student to think
about certain aspects of the past which may alert
him to discuss this phase with the family and there-

fore may lead to a comparison with what it is now.

The Family Prior to the Separation

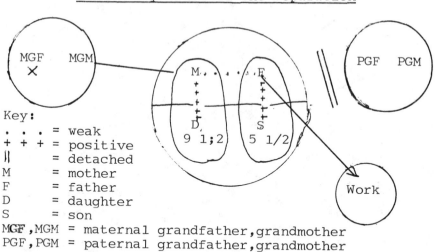

Key:
. . . = weak
+ + + = positive
|| = detached
M = mother
F = father
D = daughter
S = son
MGF,MGM = maternal grandfather,grandmother
PGF,PGM = paternal grandfather,grandmother

Of course it is essential to inquire about the
other important systems, for example, the grandparents, uncles, aunts, etc. This is especially important when dealing with incomplete and overburdened
systems. Both of these suffer from a built-in imbalance, whether it is due to a missing family member
or to a child who needs more than the ordinary care.
The above diagram reflects the hypothetical assumption
that even before the split the marriage was weak (this
is probable) and there may have been some existing
polarization between genders, i.e., the daughter was
mother's girl and the son was dad's boy. The reason
for this speculation lies in the fact that the daughter becomes the parental child, moving into the space
vacated by the father and the boy becomes the problem
child, possibly because he had lost his friend and
ally. Furthermore, he was left as the only "male" in
the family. Though the rest of the family may have
reacted to the loss, the mother with anger and the
daughter not even daring to air her feelings of missing her father lest she hurt her mother's feelings,
the position of the little boy is different. His
"aloneness" is especially marked: he not only lost
his father but, in a way, a sibling as well and, perhaps, his mother, whose little boy he once was.

Naturally, there are many other treatment tools.
Some of these are more, others less appropriate for
teaching and training purposes. Nevertheless, they

124

should be mentioned to students as useful adjuncts for family treatment. (Outside of the use of audio- and videotape to which we have already referred on various occasions, and therefore need not be discussed again) there are "family photographs", "family drawings", "family games", all of which elucidate special facets of family relationships. The first two have in common the possibility to bring back and/or correct views a person may have of his family, including his own position within the family, which may be in contrast to the stereotypical picture he may carry within himself. Family games on the other hand are devices in which family members can engage with one another so that the family therapist has an opportunity to study transactional patterns and behavior on which he then can base his treatment intervention. Certain families benefit from the sharing of fantasies and even dream material. It was previously stated how an induced fantasy can be used with students to imagine how it would be if their family (present or of origin) would enter family treatment.

The acquisition of new tools and techniques, like the expansion of skills, never ends for either the therapist or the educator. It would be presumptuous to assume that one or two semesters of teaching family therapy could in any way convey the depth and richness existing in the field. Nor can it be sufficient to make full-fledged "family therapists" out of students. However, it can create the basis for good practitioners and, with the help of appropriate supervision, it can turn out respectable helpers after graduation. As do clinicians, teachers will, of course, select those techniques that most closely reflect their basic orientation. Nevertheless, beyond this, teachers in their roles as academicians, need to constantly stress the basic issues underlying the topic. They also must inform the students of their subjective biases and at least mention opposing and controversial issues existing in the field.

REFERENCES

1. a) Haley, J.(ed.), Changing Families, New York: Grune & Stratton 1971.

   b) Minuchin, S., Families and Family Therapy, Cambridge, Mass.:Harvard University Press 1974.

2. Satir, V., Peoplemaking, Palo Alto, Cal.:Science and Behavior Books, Inc. 1972.

3. Constantine, L., "Family Sculpture and Relationship Mapping Techniques" in Journal of Marriage and Family Counseling, April 1978.

4. _____, op.cit.

5. Aponte, H., "The Family School Interview: An Eco-structural Approach" in Family Process, September 1976.

CHAPTER VIII

FAMILY THERAPY TRAINING - APART FROM ACADEMIA

Thus far we have discussed how family therapy can
be taught within the academic setting. There are,
however, many other settings in which clinicians are
trained; most of these specializing in one or another
treatment approach. The condition for admission to
these training centers is the possession of some basic
knowledge and expertise, usually a degree such as the
Master's in Social Work or an equivalent in psychology
or psychiatry. Quite different from students at the
university, trainees in institutes have already a-
chieved basic skills, but may wish to improve upon
them or to acquire some new ways of operating. Family therapy institutes, though originally aimed at
teaching this new modality to those who were ready to
make the transition from individual to family therapy,
developed and became identified with certain approaches[1] (as did their brethren in individual therapy)
which set them apart from each other.

Due to the rapid development in this field several innovative approaches have evolved: some based
on earlier foundation, others discarding some traditional precepts. others still struggling to find ways
to integrate the new and the old. Recently, several
books have been published on comparative family therapy[2]. While stressing the similarities and the differences they fail to deal with what is complementary
and what is mutually exclusive in their respective
treatment techniques. To give a specific example:
the structural therapist uses techniques aimed to
bring about change in the family through such maneuvers as tracking family sequences, making the covert
overt, or changing the structure. Many of these moves
take place in the family session. As conductor of
the session he is intensely involved. In contrast to
this the strategically oriented family therapist ex-
plores carefully and in great detail perceptions fam-

127

ily members have of at least one other dyadic relationship and in fitting various pieces together, including those which are related to significant family history, comes up with a strategy. Based on this
he gives the family various tasks to be executed at
home. He discourages discussion of this in the session, neither does he test the family's flexibility
in the session itself. In fact he often uses messages which leave the family puzzled. Direct engagement with the family is peripheral, similarly to Bow-
en's method in which the therapist is intent on staying outside the emotional field of the family.

It is obvious that some of these methods can be
combined while others can not, e.g., intense engagement and disengagement are not compatible nor is a
transaction, geared to a change in the actual situation accompanied by some comments possible, if one
aims at giving the family an unexpected prescription
at the end of a session. Some techniques of course
can be used sequentially. In fact shifting from one
method to another depending on a family's progress or
lack of it is quite customary, especially by an experienced worker-clinician.

There is a natural tendency on the part of both
seminal thinkers as well as their followers who,
while not claiming to be in possession of the ultimate
wisdom, become deeply committed to a given approach
and at times intolerant of other methods. At this
point the field of family therapy is still in the exciting period of youthful expansion and enthusiasm
with new ways being groped for and closure not yet taking place, but there is a great deal of cross-fertil-
ization occurring which enriches the field.

This chapter, however, will not describe the specific training existing in Family Therapy Institutes,
but will deal with the training of graduate social
workers in social agencies and other institutions
like hospitals where the great majority of family
practitioners is employed. Like families, these agencies have their own history and purpose; as do all
systems they both are entrenched in their past and
firmly locked into their present mode of operating.
They either serve special interest groups or offer
special or generalized services.

The relationship between these social agencies
and family therapy has an interesting history. So-

cial workers always saw the individual as an inter-
related part of the environment, and since the family is part of the environment, it has always considered the family an important adjunctive unit. It
is hardly coincidental that some agencies were called
"Family Agencies" long before family therapy was "discovered". Furthermore, home visits by social workers
have long been customary. Nevertheless, social workers like other mental health professionals became
greatly influenced by psychoanalytical concepts with
the consequence that some of the "old" practices fell
into "ill repute".

It followed that when family therapy as a new
orientation became influential in the field, a great
many social agencies found themselves still wedded to
the psychoanalytically oriented individual approach.
Thus, the need for and interest in family therapy
training became pronounced. This training is what we
will now discuss.

There are two types of training other than those
offered in family institutes and professional schools.

1. The inservice program is the type of training*
that takes place within a social agency. This can be
given either by experienced staff members or by outsiders. It is the latter to which we will address
ourselves since, if an agency has its own "experts"
able to do the teaching, it generally means that the
agency climate is favorable to what is being taught.
In fact, it may have produced its own experts. This
occurred at the Jewish Family Service, whose staff
was consistently exposed to the influence of family
therapy and contributed to its expansion.**

_____

*From now on when I refer to training I mean family
therapy training.

**One of the first clinics in which Family Therapy
was practiced was established at the former Jewish
Family Service under the joint leadership of Dr. Nathan Ackerman and Dr. Robert Gomberg, the latter having been the director of the agency. After his un-
timely death, family treatment was expanded and continued to influence the thinking and operation of the
agency which for a period of time became the leading
one in working with families. Special contributions
were made by Elsa Leichter and the author through in-
(ctd. following page)

2. The training programs offered by the community. By this I mean a program offered at a community mental health center³ or offered by a university
or sponsored by an organization such as the Family
Service Association, the American Group Psychotherapy
Association, the Association of Clinical Social Workers, etc. Universities have recently expanded their
continued educational training into Post-Masters and
Doctoral programs which gives family treatment an increasingly important place in the curriculum. The
thought underlying these programs stems from the recognition that many agencies do not have inservice
programs and that limitation can be taken care of by
intensive training seminars offered by the community.
The implicit expectation is not only to enhance the
expertise of individual staff members but for these
members to influence the agency in turn. Certain a-
gencies, in fact, encourage their staff members to
participate in such endeavors and even provide time
and sometimes funds for them. Other agencies seem to
lack such an interest but the workers seek these
learning opportunities on their own. Occasionally,
they do so even against the covert wishes of the a-
gency. Overtly, few agency executives would be a-
gainst additional training of their staff, but covert
messages are often given to staff, especially when
the newly acquired knowledge runs counter to the orientation of the agency and therefore threatens its
homeostasis!

The Inservice Training Program

This training in an agency differs from supervision. The seminar and workshop leader's responsibility is to teach a given subject matter to a group
of workers. He is not directly responsible for the
individual worker's growth and development or the detailed case management, especially in terms of its ad-
ministrative aspects. Nor is the seminar leader expected to evaluate the worker whose performance in

---

*(ctd. from preceding page)
troducing multi-family group therapy,through a novel
family oriented intake process known as "Quick Response Unit"⁴ and through the bi-agency project which
was headed by the author to avert placement of children through intensive work with their families.

the seminar is, at best, considered peripheral to
his total agency performance. Thus, it does not affect his status in the agency. Some agencies leave
it to the worker whether or not he wants to attend a
training seminar, a fact which may increase a worker's
motivation in the learning process.

When family therapy is taught in an agency not
familiar with this approach, the process usually begins with staff and administration agreeing that there
is a need to acquire a new skill, in this case, family therapy. Administration then provides the staff
members with the structure needed for learning which
includes the hiring of a consultant,allowing for time
and space and whatever teaching tools are needed by
the training person to do the job. This may include
special equipment and certain conditions such as the
availability of live families for teaching purposes.
While the practitioner assumes responsibility for his
learning, the consultant teacher has to familiarize
himself with the function of the agency, including
special rules and regulations affecting the system,
the level of knowledge of the staff, and the relative
readiness existing within the agency to let him, the
outsider, in. Thus, it is helpful for the training
person to acquaint himself, if possible, prior to
contracting with the agency, with the nature of the
"system within the system" and the process which
leads to his employment. Such knowledge will ease
the unavoidable growing pains that are likely to occur in the mutual accomodation process between the
outsider and the "in group".

Optimal learning occurs when the agency and the
consultant have the same goal. This is likely to
happen when the administration and the supervisory
staff are relatively familiar with family therapy so
that the new input can be supported by the agency
system. But, if the agency leaders are not really
familiar with what is in store for them, their participation in the learning process can help a great
deal. I have found it to be a sign that things will
go well if supervisors and sometimes even agency executives participate in the learning process.

If the supervisors do not participate in the
training process, the outer system may not only fail
to back up the new "modality" but it may unwittingly
obstruct the learning by the training group. For
instance, if the trainees begin to see whole fam-

ilies instead of just individuals and run into some unavoidable resistance and turn for help to the supervisor, they are often told that "this is not a good case for family therapy" and are directed to resume individual sessions - hence they fall back to the "old familiar". The consultant may find himself in a peculiar role: he may feel pulled between his employer and the trainees. He wants to satisfy both, but like the enmeshed family, he is stuck in an "intergenerational triangle" with split allegiance and with the overt and latent goals in contradiction. Allegiance to one is seen as "betrayal" of the other. Needless to say that in such an atmosphere integration of the new method is difficult and in extreme cases impossible.

Similarly, difficulties can also occur when the dichotomy lies in two different but interdependent departments as when family therapy is taught to the social service department of a psychiatric hospital with the psychiatric staff being individually-analytical oriented. To the extent that such differences exist the "struggle against learning the new" will more likely be projected and may be expressed somewhat like this: "WE want to work with families, but THEY don't let us". Thus, the consultant has to deal with the reality of the "hostile frightened" outer system, yet, too, has to realize that this very system provides a good hiding place for the training group's own questions, doubts and fears regarding their new undertaking. It is only when the consultant deals with both aspects, the reality and the projection, and enables the group to work on this, that differentiation and eventually some resolution can take place. Difficult as it may seem and in fact is, such process, if understood and utilized, provides a singularly rich dynamic and can lead to substantial growth.

In one setting in which I taught, a small group of social workers who were trained in family therapy eventually stimulated the interest of the "higher-ups" (who happened to be the psychologists and psychiatrists) that they eventually joined the training program.

Since some struggle is inherent in any learning process, the initial stage, not unlike the beginning phase in a class, is characterized by confusion and anxiety. In a way the process in the group is like the process in a family, which while unhappy with the status quo and eager for growth, is fearful to move toward any real change. The group will take a step forward, as does the family, only to return to the old accustomed ways if the going is rough.

Since staff members constitute a kind of "family" they bring into the group feelings related to their position and to happenings affecting their daily professional lives. In a subtle or not so subtle way, competition, hostilities, friendships and alliances are lived out in the group and often in relation to the task at hand. As in one's own family, the risk seems greater than in a group where only strangers band together. Fears of exposing one's vulnerability (for the professional it may mean one's "stupidity"), fear of showing one's real feelings, be they of anger, envy or neediness, the craving for intimacy, the fear of closeness, dependency and strivings for autonomy and independence all exist side by side.

In one of the training groups I conducted, one member who was unusually bright challenged everything I said. It became clear that she seemed driven to defeat me through obstructing the process in any way she could. She questioned my tactics, my style and the very reason for teaching family therapy. Yet whenever she could, she caught me outside of the group and assured me how much she admired me. Initially I dealt with her as the possible spokesman of the group for which she carried doubts and questions. However, as time went on and she continued, the group, possibly due to her exaggerated stance, distanced itself more and more from her. In fact it became over-positive, much as the good siblings sometimes become frightened by the bad ones in the family and through their behavior need to reassure the parents. When I focused on the existing polarity and did not permit her to control the group, she suddenly requested to leave the group. When I held her to it, she agreed and tolerated a moving engagement between herself and the group which ended with her leaving without rage. It emerged that this member had always felt herself an outsider and that she had been extremely angry with the agency and in fact with society as a whole. When she was stopped from doing this, she wanted "out"; when not permitted to act out, she was able to leave with some dignity. Several weeks later she decided to leave the agency which she had been unable to do previously due to her hostile dependent relationship.

In another training group which consisted of the
faculty of a well-known university that had gathered
to learn more about family therapy, we had first to
deal with the group members' excessive fear of exposure. Largely due to the structure in which they
worked and their status as professors, it was extremely difficult for those in the hierarchically higher
positions to show themselves as less than perfect, i.
e., all-knowing, whereas the newcomers who had lesser
status were equally afraid to show their flaws. No
member of the group was aware of the degree of irra-
tionality, since overtly they had donned the student
cap. Yet, covertly they were holding on to their
roles and positions. Once this was dealt with openly,
especially in response to my sharing with them my
fear of being judged by them and not measuring up to
my reputation, relief set in. The group grasped immediately the parallel existing between what they had
experienced and what parents often experience in the
initial family sessions in which the myth that the
parents are flawless and omnipotent is threatened.

There are occasional times when inservice training does not succeed. Sometimes in spite of an overt
desire to expose the staff to new orientation, there
is a contrary agency philosophy. This is most commonly "acted out" through shortening the period of teaching and terminating it before its seeds can take hold
among the staff. It has thus far only happened twice
in my career: once in an agency that was very committed to the psychoanalytical viewpoint and mostly
staffed by oldtimers who, understandably, were not
ready to switch their professional orientation; the
second time was in an agency whose very existence was
tied to the concept of treating the patient and not
the family. The agency's total orientation and its
program were structured in such a way that made pen-
etration of the new viewpoint difficult, to say the
least. In retrospect, I believe that I felt so defeated in both instances that I decided somewhere a-
long the line not to "pursue" the matter any further
and to remove myself from the system. I suspect this
left both the agency and myself greatly relieved.
With the benefit of hindsight, I have come to think
that I might have been more successful if I had shown
less involvement and enthusiasm and therefore would
not have overwhelmed the system so much. Perhaps if
I had adopted some sort of paradoxical approach, that

also would have freed the system for change. However, it is possible unbeknownst to me that these agencies were somehow touched by certain new thoughts which they utilized in their own way and time. This is similar to what happens in families that reject treatment, yet make progress after they lave therapy. Is it a matter of pride or autonomy?

In the majority of training experiences, the process does take hold! In my experience it usually takes from three to five years until an agency can go it alone. By this I mean that agency staff is sufficiently trained and the agency itself has made the necessary changes to accomodate to family treatment. This might include a different beginning, a holistic family intake rather than a fragmented piecemeal approach with more time, space and evening time allotted for family sessions. Agency change would mean a willingness to admit that even the "holy" custom of spacing interviews from week to week might not be advantageous to the treatment process; that blocks of time, like three-hour sessions that take place only every two or three weeks, might be more useful or manageable, especially in cases of limitations due to employment or geographical distance or other more subtle treatment related factors. Agency change could mean the use of co-therapeutic teams particularly with some perplexing families or in the case of deeply entrenched systems that tend to overwhelm the therapist. It could mean inviting a colleague for occasional participation when the therapist feels stymied or needs a hand with the family. All of these things mean influencing and even unsettling agency procedure. Therefore, they have an impact on agency structure, which, in turn, influences attitudes and behavior of the staff, as in families themselves. Staff, for instance, may be more ready to give a second evening to the agency if family sessions are recognized as requiring more time and effort and some "rewards" are given. Staff will cooperate more if it does not feel that it has to carry the entire burden. As the agency gradually shifts, an increase in the staff's working with families can usually be noted.

But, the consultant changes too. In the early phase he has to be a very active leader, a supersalesman so to speak who, in addition to having to deal with initial resistance and enabling the group to become operational, demonstrates what is possible in a given situation, often through live family inter-

views. Later, in the more advanced stages of learning the group takes on increasing importance in the
teaching process. More workers bring their own live
families into the group and do the bulk of the interviewing themselves while the consultant and the co-
workers assume an "available as needed" role. The
atmosphere changes too: from doubt to increasing
trust, from hesitation to experimentation; and gradually the consultant becomes more peripheral.

Different from the one semester academic teaching
at a university, inservice training is more case related and practice oriented. Theoretical underpin-
nings get developed more slowly and often not as extensively as they do in class situations. Moreover
the training person's special brand of family therapy
and teaching tends to be adopted by the staff, whereas in the academic setting more generic and even comparative viewpoints have to be carried.

As training goes on workers become more aware of
their own process and the role they play in helping.
Accordingly, the consultant-teacher shifts his focus
to the worker as the subject of "intervention". As
previously indicated, the worker when interviewing a
live family exposes his work to the scrutiny of the
consultant and the group. If the worker discusses a
family situation the training person needs to get a
sense as to what the worker's difficulty in a case
might be as well as to raise his own questions. In
short, the task at hand is to help the worker get
"unstuck", become more self-evaluating, objective,
etc. as the case may be.

Case Example

Recently a worker in an inservice training situation described a chaotic family whom she had treated for several months. The family consisted of parents and three children, all sons. She stated that
she felt increasingly hopeless since the family insisted in session after session that nothing changed.
This often repeated statement was in contrast with
what the worker perceived as happening. The chaotic
climate of the family in which the children had been
acting out considerably (throwing objects at their
parents even during the interviews, scapegoating the
father, fighting violently with each other - behavior
which occurred both at home, in the community and at
school) had given way to some order. The parents had

been helped to be more "in charge". The mother had been stopped from sabotaging the father through her subtle put-down maneuvers, something that the children had picked up and caricatured by means of their behavior. The mother had felt less helpless and no longer spoke of her fear of "going crazy". The family began to discuss their differences rather than acting them out and at times even found some solutions. Improved behavior on the part of the boys was reported.

Still, the worker worried about the reasons why the family insisted that therapy was not helpful. She was convinced that they would suddenly drop out and revert to their original behavior. Though I had some sense as to the "reasons" for the family's behavior, I was puzzled about the worker's discomfort. She described her discomfort graphically as a feeling she was the family's "torturer", strongly sensing their disapproval. Beyond the fact that she felt uncomfortable it was likely that this would be transmitted to the family with some adverse affect. Without of course knowing where it would lead I asked the worker to role play* a situation in her own family in which she had felt similarly. When she appeared hesitant, I repeated to her that she said that the family made her feel as if she were a "torturer". The worker then played out the following incident. At the age of 9 she was close to and quite dependent upon her older sister (12). The sister got a very bad report card and was naturally afraid of her parents' reactions. She asked "our" worker to cover up for her and to claim that the school was not giving out report cards. The truth came out and she, the worker rather than her sister, became the target of her parents' indignation for being so dishonest. She felt extremely guilty, as if she had done something really terrible, i.e., as if she had "tortured" her parents whose reproachful eyes haunted her. Yet, through it all, she knew that her intentions had been good and that she had wanted to be helpful to her sister. How could something which was good turn into something bad? Suddenly the worker relaxed, smiled and said: "oh! I know with the family I also meant well, but they always make me feel like I am doing something bad to them and that I am cruel, but I am not! The hell with their giving me recognition, I am doing OK"

---

*I am indebted to Olga Silverstein for this method

There was no need to say much. Some months later
the worker reported to the group that she had ended
with the M family soon after the group session. They
seemed to be doing well. A week before the mother
had appeared in her office, without an appointment,
and had told her that she wanted to let the worker
know that things continued to go well, in fact, that
they had improved. She added a shy "thank you" and
left.

As an unexpected by-product of this I suddenly
recalled a similar incident that occurred in my childhood. My older sister had asked me to conceal the
fact that it was "Parents' Conference Day" from our
parents for much the same reasons as were given in
the worker's childhood incident. While the "outcome"
was different: I was not blamed when it was discovered
since I was the favored child of my mother, I nevertheless felt acutely uncomfortable, split and disloyal. This feeling came back to me strongly when
the worker dealt with her feelings.

Training Programs offered by the Community

When a worker seeks additional training outside of
his agency, he is usually strongly motivated. He is
ready to invest time, money and effort in his further
training and professional future. There is some likelihood that the agency in which he works is not e-
quipped to offer the special training he is looking
for. In some instances it may not even fully approve
of the venture. While the worker does not owe any explanation about the use of his own time to the employer, he needs to get an o.k. if he is planning to use
agency material (except when used in disguised fash-
ion). This is particularly true if he plans, as is
often required by workshop leaders, to bring a live
family or a tape of a family to the group. Moreover,
if the worker hopes that his new expertise could have
an impact on the agency, it is best to discuss the
training with his superior, so that some acceptance
can be forthcoming. If this does not happen, the
worker in a training situation especially in one that
is in opposition to the agency's orientation, may find
himself in a situation that breeds conflict and dis-
content. All the difficulties which were mentioned
in the previous discussion: the lack of backing on
the part of the agency, not to speak of the lack of
supervision so necessary for any new undertaking, a

structure which may counter the worker's efforts to deal with his clients in a different way - all these are serious obstacles to learning. For instance, if an agency insists that the worker begin with the individual rather than the family group or if the worker is not allowed to include other family members afterwards, he will find himself in an impossible situation betwixt and between.

In this case, the training person is not even a "guest" of the system and the "battle" can never be fought out directly. In fact it is even difficult for the training consultant to assess whether the trainee gives an accurate account of the system he is working in. This is similar to a family in which the applicant, let us say the mother, represents the system by telling the therapist about the difficulties in the family, putting the blame upon the absent father. Without ever meeting the gentleman, not to speak of the rest of the family, the therapist will be hard put to accurately assess the degree and even the quality of the system's operation and the anti-therapeutic stance. Furthermore, the father, like the absent agency superior, becomes the ready scapegoat for anything that may go wrong. Thus, the field of transaction in which the training person (teacher) and the trainee (worker-therapist) meet each other about the salient issues of family therapy is constantly clouded by and influenced by a shadow system whose impact indeed exists, but may also be used, albeit unwittingly, to diffuse and mystify the process. The training person, in such a case, has a difficult time differentiating reality from what is perceived by the worker. Thus, messages have to be decoded on the basis of partial evidence. The same thing may occur in class when a student who does not even have the status of an employed therapist, presents agency policy or attitudes in a certain way.

Given these facts it is impressive how many students and workers have been able to carry their newly found knowledge to the agency. Often they have been able to influence the treatment policies of the agency.

REFERENCES

1. a) The _psychodynamic_ approach is still being prac-
      ticed by the Ackerman Family Institute, New
      York City, the Eastern Pennsylvania Psychiatric
      Institute, Philadelphia, Pa. and at the Boston
      Family Institute.
   b) The _structural_ school, developed and practiced
      by Dr. S. Minuchin, Philadelphia Child Guidance
      Clinic, Philadelphia, Pa.
   c) _Structural-strategic_, Jay Haley and Cloé Mada-
      nes, Family Therapy Institute of Washington,
      Washington, D.C.

   d) _Bowen_ Theory, developed by Dr. Murray Bowen,
      Family Center, Georgetown Uni. School of Med.
   e) _Strategic_ Family Therapy, first developed by
      Dr. Mara Selvini Palazzoli in Milano, Italy and
      currently practiced with some interesting modi-
      fications at the Ackerman Family Institute as
      part of a special department under the leader-
      ship of Peggy Papp and Olga Silverstein, later
      joined by Lynn Hoffman, Gillian Walker, et al.
   f) _Communication Theory_, especially used in brief
      therapy, currently practiced in the Mental Re-
      search Institute, Palo Alto, Ca., originators:
      G. Bateson and D. Jackson, now P. Watzlawick,
      J.H. Weakland and R. Fisch.
   g) _Experientially oriented_ family therapy - major
      exponent Dr. Carl Whitacker, Madison, Wisc.
   h) _Communication_ and _Growth oriented_ family ther-
      apy: Virginia Satir.

2. a) Foley, V.D., _An Introduction to Family Therapy_,
      New York:Grune and Stratton 1974.
   b) Jones, S.L., _Family Therapy, A Comparison of
      Approaches_, Bowie,Md.:Robert J.Brady Co. 1980.

   c) Paolino, T.J. and McGrady, B.S., _Marriage and
      Marital Therapy_, New York:Brunner/Mazel 1978.

3.   Flomenhaft, K. and Carter, R.E., "Family Ther-
      apy Training Program and Outcome" in _Family
      Process_, June 1877.

4.   Goldring, J., _Quick Response Therapy_, New York:
      Human Science Press 1980.

CHAPTER IX

STUDENTS AND TEACHER: A RELATIONSHIP

This chapter is more subjective than any other in this book; because it deals with the inter-relationship of students and teacher, subjectivity is unavoidable. It includes the "chemistry" between the students as a group, the individual student, and the teacher; a direct personal element that is introduced deliberately inasmuch as the discussion is based upon specific experiences the author had with the students. Some of the material used in this chapter is based on a questionnaire* which was sent to approximately fifty-five students whom I taught over a period of three years. All the students were in their last or second to last semester in Graduate Social Work at two different universities, thus in a special learning phase.

It should be noted that any classroom is characterized by a structural uniqueness since it consists of two systems - the teacher system and the student system, brought together for a given purpose within a given time span. The purpose that links them is the educational enterprise that predetermines the transactional process which takes place between the students and the teacher. It can be diagrammed in the following way:

---

* See Exhibit I, the questionnaire and the letter sent to the students. It should be noted that from the 55 letters sent out 22 questionnaires were filled out, 18 letters came back marked addresses unknown and 15 letters were not responded to. In the letter the students were asked not to identify themselves but several did.

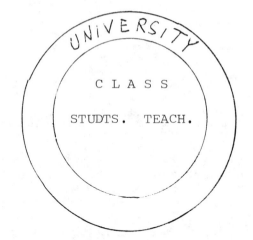

UNIVERSITY

C L A S S

STUDTS.   TEACH.

As can be seen class links students and teacher.
Teacher and students have different roles. They influence each other and are in turn influenced by the
superstructure - the university which in turn is part
of society at large. Society affects the student
body in terms of the kind of students entering the
university (fewer or more minority students, for instance); the university through the subject matter
that is being taught, the sequence which is being followed and the selection of the teachers. The teacher,
no less than the student, is exposed to these influences. In addition, the student system brings its
own "past" to the actual learning situation. Each
student comes from a family, has achieved a certain
developmental maturation level, minimally young adult-
hood. Many students of social work enter graduate
school at a much later point in life. This means
that they are at a different developmental stage than
the majority of the students. Those students have
more experience in living. They have passed more
transition points and in all likelihood have had to
cope with more life crises. Older students are
viewed with some awe and respect by their younger colleagues, not so much because of their age but because
of the "guts" it takes to return, once again, to a
learning situation and carry a student's role. Older
students may often be experienced as different and
not quite belonging to the "student group". Naturally
the older students have feelings about the younger
ones, so that this group within the larger group op-

142

erates like any other sub-group in a distinctive, often patterned way. A similar situation exists if there is a small group of minority students in the class or a handful of men, etc. The teacher should utilize these important facts in the learning process.

Students are tied to their families in a variety of subtle ways and often overestimate the degree of separation and differentiation they have achieved. Family therapists and those who teach family therapy have a sound respect for the "invisible loyalties"[1] that tie family members together, even if they are geographically separated. They are aware of the patterns existing in all of us that get transmitted over generations and tend to get incorporated and lived out. That is why the awareness of one's own place in one's family and the respective impact family members have upon each other, including significant life roles and positions become part of the curriculum in family therapy.*

The students' attitude is also affected by the sum total of his learning experience thus far. While his early learning patterns, including attitudes to authority (i.e., the teacher) may have changed considerably from grade school to graduate school in line with his development, certain attitudes tend to cling. For example, the desire to be "fed" which I jokingly call the "open mouth syndrome" or to have two contradictory demands fulfilled at the same time. (This desire, of course, has complementary aspects in the teacher himself, who wants to be the "all-giver", and, of course, knows that he cannot or should not be that, especially if he has convictions regarding the importance of the group's participation).

Students have also been exposed to a certain teaching style which colors their expectations and behavior. For instance, if the student was accustomed to group process (the emphasis on the group as an important factor in the learning process) he may expect the same from the family therapy class, or he may want just the opposite. One student indicated

---

*One of my students commented: "being a daughter and being a mother of a daughter is a unique and wonderful place to be. My professional and personal life revolves around family".

that due to the fact that he was placed in a family institute in which group process and experiential learning was dominant he wanted straight didactic learning from my class. His hope had been to get a neatly organized system of concepts. (This very student, however, unaware of the inherent contradiction, criticized the lack of intimacy in our class and compared it unfavorably to the small group he had been placed in with his agency!)

Certain students are terribly sensitive to the possibility of being "analyzed" by their teachers. They indicate that they had been exposed to much of this in their classes. These students become watchdogs regarding the fluid line between "becoming therapists" and "being in therapy". They fight against what they perceive as the analyzing of their motives or their unconscious. They tend to confuse observations of the here and now and inquiries as to a feeling, with the instructor's meddling into their personal lives.* I try to differentiate between being in touch with one's feelings in a given situation, or with one's feelings due to a position or role one has carried in either the family of origin or in the present one, from the "free-for-all confessional" regarding certain facts about one's personal life. I often say that "I am not particularly interested whether you are divorced, have mentally ill members in your family, or have any other difficulty". What is germane is the student's ability to recognize what it may feel like to be the younger sibling, or the scapegoat, the loner or the leader in the family. In fact some of the exercises introduced by me are to enable students to put themselves into the kind of experiences which are alien to them (like being the mother of a host of children who are all pulling at her) in order to be able to identify certain feelings and resulting attitudes. Some students know these

---

*See Journal of Education for Social Work, Fall '66, p. 42 in the article "Creative Adult Learning and Teaching, Who's the Engineer of the Train?" by M. M. Foeckler and G. Boynton. They comment on the same phenomenon when they state, "Whenever possible the teacher will use the students' previous experiences, current situations and interests to illustrate the learning process, the issues at hand". They refer to the students' anxiety that such information "is outside the learning task. Is it therapy or learning?"

feelings only too well and are able to share them with their colleagues. This occurs most frequently in the ending process. Of course, I try to be sensitive to the students' need for privacy, especially in the relatively impersonal setting of the university. In a training situation a similar fear over loss of privacy can even be heightened by the fact that trainees "live together" in the agency family and are afraid of certain repercussions if they reveal too much of themselves. Awareness of this fact often leads to increasing openness in the group. Occasionally it leads to even greater freedom in the agency at large.

I share with my students rather quickly and matter-of-factly the knowledge that I am divorced and have raised a daughter as a single parent. Also, I will add that I have developed a revulsion to having my home referred to as a "broken" one. I consider it, while incomplete, not "broken" at all, but rather possessing its own wholeness. My sharing this with a class should not be interpreted as a "come-on" for others but an attempt to "untaboo" various subject matter, as well as to be myself as much as possible. Freedom on the part of the teacher creates freedom on the part of the student and vice versa. Of course, the aim of any teacher is to create an atmosphere of freedom and trust for optimal learning.

There is another element that affects students in family therapy classes. It has to do with the emphasis on the part of the family therapy instructors to have their students work with families in their field work practice. If they do not have this opportunity they usually feel, and indeed are, at a disadvantage. These students tend to feel left out more frequently and, generally, are less at ease and contented than their more fortunate colleagues. Their anger is often directed at the agency which they perceive as depriving them of an opportunity, although sometimes the anger is expressed toward their colleagues and the teacher, albeit in a more subtle way. As already indicated, some students have been able to convince their agencies (sometimes with the help of the university) to allow them to experiment with an occasional family session, even though the particular agency may not be familiar with this way of working or even be negatively disposed toward it.

Nonetheless, since experimental learning is not

the same as learning through experience, the author's teaching approach offers these students a chance to do substantial learning as well. It gives them the chance to develop a conceptual framework for family therapy which can be later translated into actual doing when the opportunity arises. Role playing and working on one's own family are two very helpful tools. Also helpful is the exposure to the experience of one's colleages and, of course, the direct demonstration that occurs in class. Beyond this there are some other devices such as that developed by Murray Bowen who proposes that the therapist attempt to influence the family system by coaching an individual family member, after assessing what the system is all about. Rather than only staying with the individual client's perception the interviewer can inquire how a transaction takes place, who participates directly and indirectly and what incident preceded the action, including what words were used by whom and how the other participants would describe what occurred if they would be the informants. Thus the complexities of transactions and sequences become highlighted including their usual circulatory character. Symbolic stand-ins like an "empty chair"* or the worker taking on the role of another person contribute to the emergence of quite realistic scenes.

We have already discussed what influences students' attitudes and behavior and what each student brings to the experience as being uniquely his own. Now we will explore in greater depth their coping patterns in class, which is the external agent through which the teacher perceives them.

While students can be classified in a variety[2] of ways the author finds it helpful to differentiate them in the following way:

Active	Passive
Positive	Positive
Negative	Negative

---

*A well-known exercise borrowed from Gestalt Therapy

a) The Active-Positive

Active-positive students show a high degree of overt involvement, they tend to articulate what they feel and think. They help the learning and group process through their risk taking and active participation. They listen well to others and tend to be stimulated by their colleages' output. While they are usually interested in and even enthusiastic about the subject matter, they allow themselves to differ with the instructor and challenge him appropriately. Thus, in a way, they are natural regulators of the teaching process. If there is only one or two of this type of student in a class, the teacher may exploit them. He/she may make them into the parental child of the class family. In such a case what is basically positive can turn into something noxious. This can be minimized, by making the process overt or by working with the group on the phenomenon itself.

b) The Active-Negative

The active-negative student is equally verbal and articulate as the AP student. He, too, usually has leadership qualities and takes risks. At times he is very helpful to the group since he is often the expressor for the negative which if not brought to the surface may go underground. Or, he may be an enthusiastic forerunner into areas that are frightening to the class because they are new. For example, he will be enthusiastic about family therapy at a point when the rest of the students are still struggling to "accept" the modality of he might offer a live family too quickly, before the process has been lived through. In the latter case he may also be seen as the "teacher's pet", especially if the teacher, for whatever reason, allies himself with the active-negative student. However, different from his AP colleagues he is not well attuned to the process of the class. Nor is he in touch with the needs and level of his colleagues or, sometimes, of the teacher. If left unchecked he may become a monopolizer regardless of the positive or negative stance he chooses to take. If it becomes a problem for the class, one has to deal with this like any other class phenomena.*

---

*As will be seen when the questionnaires are analyzed, several students felt that the author as a (ctd. on following page)

c) The Passive-Positive (the quiet learner)

The passive-positive student is visibly involved,
but he conveys his involvement primarily through non-
verbal communication. (An attentive look, non-verbal
responses like smiles, body posture, etc.) He is not
likely to be the first to volunteer, but if requested,
he responds and often comes through in a meaningful
way. He is aware of and occasionally unhappy about
his reluctance (difficulty) to participate directly.
He tends to envy his colleagues who are more vocal in
the process. Nonetheless, there are students of this
type who have accepted their learning pattern. They
know that they learn through observation and they do
their best thinking in private.* In contrast to the
previously mentioned student types, these students
are satisfied and do not wish to change. The passive-
positive student is essential for the homeostatic
balance of the class, no less than his more active
peers. While not leading, this student is acutely
aware of others and tends to be sensitive and thought-
ful in his class contributions. As a teacher it is
hard to differentiate between the passive-positive
student who prefers to be left the way he is and the
one who yearns to be encouraged, to be "brought out".
Several students in their spontaneous comments in the
questionnaire have either apologized for or regretted
not having participated more overtly. Others insisted
that they felt good about the way they operated and
were a bit dismayed that I did not appreciate their
style. They thought that I would have preferred it
had they "shown more of themselves". I plead guilty
to this, yet as of now I still have not found a way,

----

*(ctd. from preceding page)
teacher tended to fall into this trap, at least in
one of the classes. She was criticized for not dealing appropriately with it. It is possible that she
mistook the AN students for AP students.

*One of my students called himself an "attentive
learner". He put it thusly: "I am not overtly active, but I listen and absorb not because of fear or
risk. Maybe this style is not fully appreciated by
the teacher!"

within the brief period of a semester, to develop e-
nough sensitivity to enable me to differentiate between those PP's who want to be helped to become more
articulate and those who prefer to be left alone.

d) The Passive-Negative

The passive-negative student acts in, not out!
He will not make his questions overt, nor verbally
give vent to his doubts, dissatisfactions or disa-
greements. He often sits silently, almost sullenly
in class and if he sends out messages they will be
disquieting to the teacher. When asked to articulate
these messages, he will deny his behavior. He prefers
to skip classes or to drop out in an efforts to avoid
direct confrontation. This student neither trusts
the teacher nor the rest of the students. He generally keeps to himself. At times he forms an alliance
with another kindred student. If he does this, he
and his friend tend to act together, sometimes whis-
pering in class or forming other visible coalitions.
While this kind of behavior, especially in its extreme form, only rarely happens to me, or to most
teachers I would assume that my reaction to it, when
it occurs, would be of helpless annoyance, particularly after I have tried to reach the student in various ways. Moreover I feel suspicious of what the PN
student is up to. In one instance, in which such a
student dropped out, I tried to reach her at home on
several occasions. I left messages and finally wrote
her a letter, all without any response.

There are various ways in which a teacher can get
a sense of how his students feel about a class, if by
class we mean the interplay between teacher and student, students among each other, subject matter and
the teaching approach employed. Each of these components plays an important role and either aids or hin-
ders the learning process. In the last analysis, the
most significant measurable component is related to
what and how much a student has learned in the course.
Thus, his comprehension of the subject matter and his
ability to utilize this comprehension in practice is
the measure of a course's and, therefore, a teacher's
success.

Nevertheless, since I believe that certain components in the process of learning are pertinent to the
goal, I used the responses to the questionnaire to
check on my impressions and to give the students a

149

chance to express their own thoughts.

Their responses illuminate the relationship between such intangibles as the feeling existing between
students and teacher, amongst the students themselves,
the class atmosphere, the degree of stimulation experienced by the students as well as their sense of a-
chieving the ultimate goal.

Since the responses fall into certain patterns
they give a fairly accurate view of how the students
regard the teaching process, and how they perceive
the teacher as a person with his own assets and lia-
bilities. I have tried to classify and analyze the
returns and have attempted to include some verbatim
comments to illustrate a point or a particular student's feelings or perceptions, leaving the student's
own words intact.

Some questions fall into a relatively factual category. For instance, the students were asked to label
and describe the teaching approach, their perception
as to the most important thing they experienced, and
the most important thing they had learned. They were
also asked to rate the kind of teaching areas they
were exposed to and had benefited from. Finally,
they were asked whether their attitudes had changed
in regard to family therapy and to state if they
felt in the end "more" or "less" competent in their
practice.

On a more subjective level the students were
asked to describe their feelings in class and to
state whether, and under what circumstances, they
changed, to appraise the atmosphere that existed in
class, and the feelings they had regarding their
peers, to rate their own ability to take risks. They
were asked to assess the teacher and describe weaknesses and strengths. It should be noted that the
possibility of criticism was inherent in several of
the aforementioned questions and in the comments many
students added. While in many ways they were extremely positive, the students seemed quite free to
be critical, and I find it particularly rewarding
that some of the criticism fell into similar paterns,
thus carrying more validity than the purely idiosyncratic criticism.

My teaching approach was almost unanimously described as experiential, dynamic, using the "here and
now", teaching through examples, role playing and live

150

families. Several students commented that "we learned within the living context", "issues were tied together while the major focus was maintained and the
needs of the class responded to". Others spoke of
the emphasis on process but related to content and
called the approach direct and confrontative, the
teacher using herself as a role model", "inquisitive,
challenging, self-revealing, probing and socratic".
Another student described the approach as "flowing
from participants' questions to concepts to method",
and yet another said "combination of theory and practice - came together in a beautiful synthesis". Some
described the teacher rather than the approach, calling her "warm and open and accepting differences
though holding to her convictions about family therapy". On the critical side it was stated that there
was not enough "didactic material". Two students
thought that the teaching was too student-centered
and was more led by the students than the teacher.

In response to question # 3 in which the students
were asked to rate what area of learning was most developed with a rating of (1) standing for the most,
(2) as intermediary and (3) as the least important,
the table below will show the average rating for each
category:

Process	1.53
Technique	2.00
Self-awareness	1.94
Family Awareness	1.61
Content	2.47

As can be seen the lowest and therefore the most important rating was given to Process, the next, following closely, was Family Awareness. Self-awareness
and Technique were group together and they were seen
as having an intermediate value. By far the least important to the respondents was Content with an average rating of 2.47. Percentage-wise and numerically,
the table looks this way:

	N	No.	1 %	No.	2 %	No.	3 %
Process	19	11	58%	6	32%	2	11%
Technique	19	4	21%	11	58%	4	21%
Self-awareness	18	7	39%	5	28%	3	33%
Family Awareness	18	10	56%	5	28%	3	17%
Content	17	2	12%	5	29%	10	59%

Questions # 4 and # 7 are related and deal with
the most vital experience the student felt he had had
in class and to mention the three most important
things he had learned in the course. Unanimous feeling was expressed that the live family demonstration,
including the process related to it was by far the
most important experience they had had. Comments conveyed a high degree of enthusiasm. Here are some of
them: "the live family interview brought all the theories to life and because of the emotional involvement
of the observers will not easily be forgotten". "This
experience brought home techniques which no amount of
reading could have replaced". "The interview was mag-
nificent. It felt like an artist must feel when he
views a Monet". "The live interview tied a lot of
previous learning together. It was inspiring and influenced my work with families subsequently". The
student who had brought the family commented: "It
gave me lots of material to work with with the family
thereafter". There was also considerable appreciation expressed for the process in relation to the actual interview including the strategy session and the
post-consultation session. One student put it this
way: "The live interview and the whole process made
family therapy come alive in a new way and seeing the
therapist work made the process less intimidating".
I consider this statement especially interesting in
the light of the frequently expressed feeling that
students are so awed by the performance of the consultant therapist that they become more intimidated.
Not one student mentioned feeling this way. Tapes
were rated as second in importance but far less often
than the live interview itself. The responses to the
three most important things learned were more varied.
Many students stressed that they gained a better understanding of the system and were able to see that
family dysfunctioning was as much rooted in the family as in the individual. They mentioned family
therapy from a developmental point of view and the
impact of other systems on the nuclear family. The
use of self-awareness and family awareness and the
need to be active as well as the importance of direct
observation of the process and techniques facilitat-
ingintervention were mentioned by many. Techniques
such as making the "covert overt", the opening up of
secrets and taboos and establishing connecting links
were among those cited. The working with process and
interaction, making empathetic connections in the
here and now and restructuring tasks were also seen
to be helpful to their work with families.

As to question # 2 about feelings experienced in
class, students generally spoke about a high level of
excitement, interest, stimulation and inspiration.
Some added that they felt overwhelmed and at times irritated and frustrated (see later). They attributed
the exciting feelings to their watching the process
unfold, their becoming increasingly clear and challenged and ready to take risks. A few marveled at
how much had been learned in so short a time. A substantial number felt anxiety and confusion, especially in the beginning phase. Certain students felt intimidated. One student was quite explicit in her
criticism when she described an incident in which I
had taken over for the role-playing student, who was
a friend of hers, with apparent disregard of the other student's feelings. A more general criticism was
directed against students who took too much of the
instructor's time to a point that some of the respondents felt temporarily bored or frustrated. Criticism of the teacher is, of course, implied in this
case. An occasional student objected to my too positive stance in regard to family therapy: "If she
believes in it why does she have to stress it so
much!" Another objected to my not giving sufficient
time to comparing various family therapy approaches.
These feelings, nevertheless, were described as being
of a temporary nature and in regard to specific incidents. Apparently they did not prevent the students from feeling enthusiastic and morivated.

The most controversial area had to do with the
students' feelings about their peers and the group
situation, Question # 8. One could speculate that
this may be related to some preference students have
for the dyadic situation. The same need may be met
when the teacher uses the lecture style (the class
then becomes one symbolic person who receives what
the instructor gives). I suspect, however, that it
reflects a so far unresolved dilemma on the author's
part, who sometimes vacillates between the group's
needs and the importance of the group process and
her responsibility as a teacher to provide information and skills. Ideally these pulls should be integrated. Personally, I find it an exciting though
never-ending struggle to maintain a balance. Yet,
from the students' vantage point this can be seen at
times as getting out of kilter. A slim majority of
students felt very inhibited in the group, afraid to
take risks, although most of them became more confident and daring as time went on. One student explained

her decrease in fear thusly: "It was due to the teacher's accepting attitude and support of those who were off base while she never relinquished her position of guidance in pulling things together". Another student stated that her anxiety decreased markedly when she experienced the excitement and enthusiasm of the group ... she related how, when she finally opened up in class, her peers received her contributions so positively that she felt even better.

Several students, a distinct minority, felt very differently about the situation. They saw some students driving the instructor "off course", which hindered their integration. Others regretted that there was not more input into the process from the quiet students, and thought role-playing or discussing the matter of the silent students might have helped. The fiercest criticism was voiced by three students. It had to do with their irritation about certain students repeatedly describing their work as "beautiful"; they perceived the teacher as being in collusion with these students, evidenced by the fact that she did not stop them.

About half the students felt that the teacher-student balance was right, that they had learned from their peers as they had from the teacher herself. "The atmosphere in the class was trusting and gave me confidence. I felt free to speak and ask questions and keep quiet without feeling pressured". "A lot of learning took place among peers. The learning was vertical and horizontal. The open, accepting atmosphere made the family therapy class the high point at school". I suspect, though I cannot be certain, that the particularly critical voices mentioned earlier belonged to members of one class where two students really almost "killed" the process by their enthusiasm. Obviously, I was still dependent on some positive input about family therapy which was not forthcoming from the rest of the students (indeed, how could it if the few were so over-enthusiastic!) and I leaned too hard on these two students, allowing them to become monopolizers, hampered the process, and probably polarized the class unduly. Yet, even in this class most students eventually learned to participate more fully.

As to Question # 9, what my students liked most and stated most frequently was: "warmth, caring, honest, risk-taking, humor and vitality". The de-

154

scriptive terms used most often were "dynamic, ex-
uberant, deeply invested and committed to teaching
and the subject matter". At times, I was also rated
as "impatient" and, by one student, described as "ir-
ritatingly nervous". Knowledge and expertise and
skill were highly acclaimed, although a few students
desired more and others less experiential teaching.
The readiness to listen to other people's viewpoints,
openness and respect for other ideas was contrasted
by certain students who felt that I was too enamored
by family therapy and too student centered. One student admired "her ability to work instantaneously
with a class happening" and"to make it a learning experience, to generalize from the specifics so that material could be conceptualized". Another stated that
the teacher was: "a great improviser in the use of
self and had the ability to perceive multiple messages". However, some students felt that I tried to
cover too much in the given time span. A few were
bothered by my diction and accent. A few found that
I played favorites with a couple of students while
failing to encourage others. A final comment had to
do with the lack of organization, despite the fact
that the student added he nevertheless learned from
direct observation. Several students were moved by
the care shown in comments on their final assignments.

I have left for the end of the responses questions
that have to do with the achievement of the essential
aim in any practice related teaching, namely the ability to translate the newly acquired concepts into action (treatment) and the degree of competence experienced by the student. Since working with families,
in contrast to working with individuals, requires a
"second order change" in the way that the student looks
and deals with human problems, one of the questions
asked in the questionnaire had to do with change of
attitudes, i.e., Question # 5. The other had to do
with the degree of competence that the student felt,
i.e., Question # 6.

Practically all the students reported some change
in attitude as well as a greater degree of competence.
However, this statement was qualified by four students
who said that they felt both "more" and "less" competent at the same time. The latter seemed to come
from their awareness of how much more there was to be
learned. Even the very few students who apparently
had no family to work with felt "ready to do so now"
and one student was glad that the course helped him

155

to have his first session with a family. The change
in attitude ranged from doubting the efficacy of family therapy to becoming a "convert". Most students
spoke about a general broadening and deepening of understanding. They gave specific examples such as:
"better understanding of the system, knowing there
were no 'villains' in a family, just people caught up
in a vicious circle". Several spoke of noticing a decrease in their judgmental attitudes and a concomitant
lessening of their tendency to view people in pathological terms. One student expressed relief that
what was demonstrated was a "learnable" approach.
Those students who had come in with considerable commitment said they had gained in competence and now
had more facts on which to base their thinking.

In regard to the spontaneous comments, Question
10, I am somewhat hesitant to quote verbatim re-
marks made by various students, lest it be interpreted
by the reader as an "ego trip" for the author. Nevertheless, I have finally decided to share them: "for
somebody who had difficulties absorbing theory, the
strong use of actions and class examples were meaningful and enabled me to tie practice and theory together.
I experienced the art of practice. Friday afternoons
came to be as much an event or drama as a class and
this to me is what education is about". Another student commented: "watching you, one of the real mas-
ters, was a real gift. It enabled me to struggle
more". "I learned so much in self-awareness and grew
in my ability to observe process". "This course has
been the high point of my academic career. It was one
I never wanted to miss and one of only a few which had
true relevance to my fieldwork placement". "My own
opinion of Mrs. S. was that she overshadowed all other
instructors on campus. The big asset is that her contact with each student is so very personal that one
feels sure that student is remembered even if she is
forgotten", and, finally, "this class has been different from any other I have ever been in. It brought
my feelings to the surface! I laughed, I cried, I
felt shitty, inspired, tired, energized - this class
wiped me out". While the above remarks reflect a
great deal of enthusiasm, they also confirm that the
course in family therapy bridged the abyss between
fieldwork and academic learning.

It is interesting and not really surprising that
various students reported not only change in their
attitudes as professionals, but that they engaged in

spontaneous change vis-a-vis their own families as well!* This confirms my belief that no student or trainee in the process of becoming a family therapist can remain unaffected in terms of his own family relationships. In some cases the different perception may lead to "actions" and in others it remains within the personal sphere and only gets reflected in barely perceptible shifts of attitudes. The choice as to what to do with this difference should, in my opinion, be the person's alone.

This feeling notwithstanding, it was extremely meaningful to me when some students chose to share how their contact with family therapy had affected their personal lives. Here are a few examples: "I have been in individual analysis for years and always thought I was the 'guilty' party. In this class I learned that pathology lies in the family and in the clan. I understood the place scapegoating had in my family and I feel less guilty and function better. I gained a more positive outlook on people and am less bothered by the 'negative'".

It is quite obvious that the students' responses and comments reflect quite accurately what and how I teach regardless of whether they experienced and judged it positively or negatively. Even those students who were full of admiration were able to put out some qualifications while the most negative comments were appropriate within the context described or they were stemming from a student's particular dislike of a personality characteristic of mine. Most students indicated that the experience has enabled them to view their own family somewhat differently.

Many of the phenomena described and observations made regarding the relationship between teacher and graduate students are applicable to all institutional

---

* There are several training centers that insist that each trainee work directly with his own family, a few include family members in their training program. I do not choose to make this either a prerequisite or a primary focus of my training, but in the academic setting I feel it to be misplaced.

learning experiences. I am referring to the systems interplay (university, class and teacher), the respective roles teacher and students carry, and the implications thereof, and the student types. Inherent in the situation is the role differential between the teacher and the students based on the built-in expectation that the teacher teaches and the student learns. Differences in learning styles as well as in behavior patterns on the part of the students make for certain characteristics, as does the teacher's frame of reference, his personal style which colors a given class atmosphere. Like every teacher, I strive to find "the balance between the common goal and allow for sufficient 'adventure' to make the learning and teaching process both arduous but ever exciting".*

There are, however, two factors which have a particular influence on the teaching (learning) described: one has to do with the sequence of events and the particular subject matter, the other with the fact that the Family Therapy Class takes place either in the first or second semester of the last year which means during a period of time when the student is in a transitory period from being a student to becoming a full-fledged professional (practitioner). Concerns such as the availability of a job, trepidations as well as longing to be finally on one's own (relieved of the student's role) affect the student profoundly and need to be taken into consideration by the instructor.

The other factor relates to the sequential order of the curriculum and affects the teaching of Family Therapy equally. It is related to the fact that students during their undergraduate as well as through most of their graduate work have been exposed to a curriculum in which the individual rather than the family unit has been the focus of clinical attention in spite of some sociologically oriented courses dealing with family phenomena. The clinical orientation has been heavily influenced by psychoanalytic and ego-psychological concepts.[3] Hence, one of the major

---

*Dimensions and dynamics of engaging the Learner" by Mary Louise Somers, Annual Progress Meeting of the Council of Social Work Education, Seattle, January, 1971

158

tasks confronting the student lies in the need to exchange his "lenses": to learn to look at and examine
phenomena in a different, namely a holistic systemic
way. Thus emphasis, priorities and differences in intervention, some in digression, others in juxtaposi-
rion to what has been learned earlier has to occur.
Students deal with this in a variety of ways which
tend to intensify though not fundamentally alter their
pattern of learning. Admiration as well as angry re-
jection, silent disapproval as well as quiet confirmation reflect students coping patterns in relation to
exposure to something new and different. It is hoped
that it leads for most students to a reorientation in
thinking and eventually to the kind of integration
with substantial grounding in the subject matter to
substantiate a variety of viewpoints.

REFERENCES

1. Boszormenyi-Nagy, I. and Spark, G.M., _Invisible Loyalties_, Hagerstown, Md.:Harper & Row 1973.

2. Chickering, A.W. describes in "Developmental Change as Major Outcome" (from Keaten, N.T. and Associates: _Experimental Learning_, San Francisco: Jossey-Bass) how students learn differently; some through acquisition of information, others by dis-covering a scientific method and logical analysis and yet others by seeking new experiences, out of which they organize theoretical concepts.

3. Hanna, E.A. and Marziali, E.A., "A Direct Practice Concentration: Problems in Integration" in _Journal of Education for Social Work_, Spring 1977.

<u>E X H I B I T</u>

The questionnaire reads as follows:

(1)   How would you characterize my teaching approach?

(2)   What were some of the dominant feelings you had while in class (excitement, boredom, confusion, irritation, etc.) and did any or some of them change during the life of the class? Please describe

(3)   Please enumerate which of these areas were most extensively covered in the course (1, 2, 3, you may use the same number twice)
Content
Process
Techniques
Self-awareness
Family Awareness

(4)   What experience did you consider the most important in class and why?

(5)   Did you change your attitude toward family therapy and what contributed to this change?

(6)   If you compare the beginning and the end of the semester did you feel
$\genfrac{}{}{0pt}{}{\text{more}}{\text{less}}$ competent in conducting a family session?

(7)   State the three most important things you have learned in this course

(8)   How did you perceive your peer group and the atmosphere in which the group operated? Were you able to take risks, or were you inhibited? Did you learn from your colleagues? What is your assessment of teacher-group balance? Would you have liked
$\genfrac{}{}{0pt}{}{\text{more}}{\text{less}}$ input from your peers?

(9)   What do you consider my greatest weaknesses and assets as a teacher?

(10) Spontaneous comments.

CHAPTER X

E N D I N G

Ending is a phase experienced without full awareness of its presence and its imminence. Often one
thinks of endings only when they occur; like the
last day of school, the last class, the final goodbye.

All cultures celebrate beginnings and endings.
The rituals associated with these events convey joy
and sadness, the two most prominent feelings accompa-
nying the events of birth and death. While on some
level ending is thought of as connoting the ultimate
separation with its deathlike finality, some rituals
suggest that joy is not altogether missing from the
experience. For instance, the Irish Wake or the descriptions some profoundly religious people give when
they speak of the joyous feelings of entering another,
albeit unknown sphere of being. Recent scientific ex-
periments indicate that people who were practically
dead, but subsequently revived, reported euphoric
sensations unlike anything they had encountered previously. Conversely, the joyous events of birth and
marriage though associated with happiness often carry
some element of sadness. The birth of a child brings
to mind the coming of a new generation and therefore,
the passing of the older generation. While such
thoughts are rarely articulated, the tears of the parents of the bride (and sometimes the groom) are more
commonly accepted and more openly expressed. When
the young adult ventures out on his own and leaves
the family of origin, there is, of course, some reason for sadness as well as joy. Outside the issue of
separation, on perhaps a more hidden level, the
thought of one's mortality may enter one's mind. This
may, in part, account for some of the tears. These
are called "tears of joy" in an effort to explain the
unexplainable or that which one fears to acknowledge.
Thus, as the ending process has aspects of the beginning process, all beginning has an element of ending.

161

While it is true that separation and ending in an education setting do not have the dramatic quality of the more fundamental human events referred to above, the French saying, "Separer est un peu comme mourir"* reflects a basic psychological truth. It means that even less far reaching events evoke basic and archaic feelings in all of us, consciously or unconsciously. These feelings influence the way we feel about and deal with lesser events.

In the classroom, several weeks before the actual ending occurs, a process is set in motion that affects both students and teacher, whether either one is fully aware of its occurrence or not. Events tend to take on a new intensity and urgency. Some of this is related to external reality and some of it is due to the processes above. For students in the final semester, it means that they are ending with their clients and their own student life.** Just as students have reached a certain level of comfort in working with their client families, they have to begin to think of ending with them. Sometimes this takes place long before they have reached whatever desired goal they had set for themselves. Students who are placed in settings in which a time limited approach is used are in a better position since supervisors usually focus on the ending process. Nevertheless, if the agency is not experienced in working with families, they may not be as knowledgeable regarding the differences existing in ending with families as compared to individuals. If students are placed in settings where no specific time span is prescribed they have to evaluate whether a given family needs further work or can be helped to terminate so that the termination of the family's treatment coincides with the leaving of the student-worker himself. Transferring a family to another worker in an agency that has few or no workers available who know how to deal with families creates yet another problem. In some such

---

*"To separate is a little like dying"

**Since most family therapy courses in the Master's curriculum of social work schools are elective courses and many of them take place in the last semester, I will address myself to the ending phase of those students who are in their last term in school prior to graduation.

cases it may be more desirable to enable the families
to go out on their own and be satisfied with a limited goal with the understanding that if the need arises
in the future, they may seek additional help, perhaps
at a different resource. In a way, the student who
is in the least favorable position in relation to
terminating with his family is the one who also was
in such a position when it first came to working with
families. In both instances, the agency is not e-
quipped to provide the kind of supervision the student needs, supervision which is particularly important in the beginning and ending periods. However,
all the students have to engage in an ending process
with the client families just at the point when they
have become excited about the many possibilities that
tend to get opened up when one works with families.
There is rarely sufficient time in class to deal with
specifics of a given family. Yet, whenever possible,
there are some points that I try to make, although
never exhaustively due to time limitations.

Informing the Family

It is essential to let families know well in advance of the prospective leaving of the student-worker. This is exactly what all therapists would do
with their individual clients. This may or may not
coincide with the termination of treatment although
it may eventually lead to it. There are two factors
involved: one has to do with the worker's leaving,
the other has to do with where the family stands in
treatment. Both have a profound influence on each
other. The fact that an end is imminent may have
considerable impact on a person's or a family's mobi-
lization. Everyone who has worked in an ending process or in a time limited approach is familiar with
this phenomenon. That which creates anxiety can also
be energizing and mobilizing. Similar dynamics are
played out in the learning process.

Simultaneously with the speeding up process that
may take place, there is a counter dynamic which is
more threatening and unsettling to the student-worker
and the family. This can be observed when a family
member or the total family reverts to earlier behavior
under the stress of the impending separation. For instance, if the family was organized around a symptomatic child, it may once again be this child who gives
distress signals reflecting in all likelihood the
anxiety state of the family. On the other hand, if

the difficulties were expressed in the inter-personal
area as in a marital feud, the couple may revert to a
level of earlier immature squabbles. Small wonder
that the student-worker tends to feel even more defeated than in the beginning. Indeed, if after a
short spurt of improvement, the family does regress,
the student tends to doubt the "reality" of the progress. His anxiety and disappointment is likely to
be picked up by the family itself, feeding their own
doubts. When these potential developments are discussed in class, students usually feel relieved and
are quickly able to help the family "live through"
the upheaval of the ending. While the symptom may be
the same as the one with which the family had originally come for help, the underlying reasons are different. The family uses their customary S O S signal
because they find themselves in a stress situation.
The difference lies in the fact that the family is
now attempting to deal with separation and the necessary reorganization of the system that prepares itself for the worker's exodus. In a way, it can be
compared to what a family goes through when the death
of one of its members is imminent (or other forms of
drastic separation) or, in a less traumatic situation,
when one child leaves for college. To the extent
that the family will be able to express and deal with
what really is ailing them, the family is less likely
to choose other means of expressing themselves and
hence "acting out" is less probable. In fact, the
successful resolution of this crisis may well aid the
family in later similar crises.

In contrast to the way it operated in the beginning phase, the family is generally better equipped
at the moment the student-worker leaves. Whatever was
learned has in some way become incorporated into the
system by then. The family also has a considerable
advantage over the individual who, for all intents
and purposes, is left to manage on his own. He really
IS deserted. On the other hand, the family, while
allowing the therapist to become part of their lives,
rarely becomes completely dependent upon the family
therapist as an individual frequently does in a dyadic relationship. One of the major reasons for this is
related to some phenomena and interventive moves which
have already been discussed. The family therapist at
best is a temporary stand-in whether he functions as
an ally, model or facilitator for another family member or sub-group. As was pointed out earlier, the
less the family therapist takes over and the more the

family is encouraged to do for itself, the more
strength and know-how the family gains. This strength
does not lie within a given member but in the unit,
expressed in a combination of actions and attitudes
that may emanate from various members in the family.
For instance, as the family learns to listen to each
other and read each other's distress signals, finds
ways to solve problems together, it will become a family which has learned to cope better. Since the family therapist addresses himself more to a dysfunctioning area than to a dysfunctioning person, each person
contributing to the malfunctioning will be encouraged
to change (do something differently), hence there
will be more built-in alternate ways of managing. In
any family that has made some progress, this will
have begun to occur. Thus, even without the family
therapist's presence certain gains may well be sus-
tained. More specifically since the ending with the
worker is something that is being lived through with
the entire family, the family unit will be better e-
quipped to deal with the pain of separation, the anxiety of the unknown, even though some members may experience lighter, positive feelings in relation to
this event. The quantity and quality will, of course,
vary depending on the type of family that the student
deals with, the difficulties they find themselves in,
and how far along in the process they have come. In
fact, the ending process, as previously mentioned, is
an opportunity to deal better with all life contingencies that have to do with separation.

The focus in the class discussion is on what is
likely to happen in the ending period, both to the
family and to the student-worker and how best to deal
with it. Students have reached a greater awareness
of family dynamics and processes by this time. They
are further cognizant of how they as a group can help
each other through identification, exchange of experience, thoughts and ideas. The student's contributions usually reflect a characteristic of the ending
phase, namely a level of integration which has not
been in evidence prior to this time. It is different
from the expecting passivity of the initial stage and
different from the vital struggle of the middle as
well. While some students go back to certain questions they posed initially regarding the purpose and
character of family therapy that may sound as if they
were reverting to the beginning, the questions are
less challenging or rhetorical, more conceptualized
and yet more specific; to ask the right question is

almost better than to find the correct answer. Most importantly, it is the group that more often than not deals with these topics. The instructor can afford to let the class handle it, more than at any other phase of teaching. A sentence here or there seems sufficient to get the class back to the issues at hand. Therefore, while the class spirit shows a heightened level of intensity, the level of knowledge and ability of the class to function as a group reflects greater responsibility and autonomy.

Some anxiety on the part of the students is also expressed in their reference to and inquiry regarding the final and only written assignment.

The students can choose between two assignments: the first deals with an actual family which the student treated while the second addresses the student's own family. The inherent difficulties in the latter have to do with the formulation of the assignment itself in which the student is asked to be subjective (relate feelings and thoughts he has had regarding his position in the family). Yet in the second part of the paper he must be objective, as the therapist would be. In their attempt to be objective, some students cannot allow themselves to be direct in the sharing of very personal feelings regarding incidents in their lives. For those who can do this and the assignments are often filled with agony, the reward lies in the growth inherent in looking at one's own family in a way the writer has previously never quite done and in the feelings that this process may release. A few found it so difficult that they simply could not complete the assignment. They were given permission to write about another family they had known intimately. These papers never carry the immediacy of the ones which deal with real life or with their own families.

An excerpt of the first type of assignment shows how observant a student can be regarding a non-verbal transaction in a family session as well as how skillfully and sensitively he dealt with a family. Here the focus is on sibling interchange in a family headed by the mother (husband divorced) in which the problem child, Kevin (the scapegoat) is the one whose unacceptable differences in part related to his being pro the divorced father. Jack, the oldest, the Parental Child, reviews the history of the absent father's forgotten birthdays and broken promises:

As the youngest echoes and elaborates his charges,
Jack passes them pieces of candy, ignoring Kevin
during this interchange. As this occurs mother
remains silent, appearing to be curled up in her
seat, carefully measuring each word of assault directed toward the absent father; finally she begins to laugh nervously and blurts out "you people
are really with it". The charges, although probably not unfounded, seem to be well rehearsed.
Kyle, the youngest, seems to soliloquize and at
one point, when the subject has changed, he in-
terrupts anxiously with "another way in which
Daddy has hurt me" as if to solidify his position
with the others. As all of the foregoing unfolds,
Kevin is slumped in his chair with outstretched
legs and head bowed. Jack asks his brother if he
thinks "Daddy loves him" and Kevin responds "yes"
and becomes befuddled and irritated at Jack's subsequent cross examination. Jack, Sean and Kyle
began to talk about Kevin as "he" and they began
to reflect on what "he feels" so I assigned the
task of speaking directly to the person who is being referred to and checking out how he feels
rather than speaking for that person. This is a
restructuring intervention in that it provides a
challenge for the system to change. This changed
the interactions in that they began to face one
another when they spoke; thus Kevin was drawn in,
even if in disagreement. This set the stage for
the initial confrontation between Jack and Kevin:

Jack: (seated directly across from Kevin) "Do
    you think Daddy loves you?"
Kevin: (sits up) "yes"
Jack: "What has he done to show you, has he
    taken you any place, called you, brought
    you anything... etc."
Kevin: (slumps down in his chair, has no
    answer, gains no support, seems to feel
    misunderstood)
Worker: (as if to reflect what the others are
    feeling). "It's hard to believe what
    Kevin is saying after being as hurt as
    you've all been, it's just hard to un-
    derstand" (there is a pause while the
    others are nodding in agreement, and
    then I address Kevin). "You have warm
    feelings for your dad which are unex-
    plainable, yet they're there!"
Kevin: (sits up) "that's right".

The second assignment often deals with a family event in the student's past, although some rare students have the courage to describe a current, not yet resolved event in their final paper. Others use comments made by the author, when she returns the paper, to mobilize themselves in directions in which they had not been able to move in the past. One student stated how she finally found the strength to "refuse her home to her alcoholic son". Another student stimulated by my commenting on her too rational approach when she described the institutionalization of her younger severely retarded sister, an event which had taken place long ago, decided to visit her with her husband. This was a "first" in her marriage and it enabled the couple to experience together an area of old pain which the student had not dealt with in her adult years.

In a recent paper a student, the middle-aged father of two children, described his family as placing high value on achievement. He and his wife took considerable pride in their successful children. Suddenly they were confronted with their older daughter's delinquency. In what must have been a gruelling process, the student while writing this paper began to see his family in a different light. He began to see that the qualities that they had valued so deeply, namely their kindness, their goodness, their being so rational and "ever-understanding" were, in part, a facade in which they had all colluded to avoid a struggle related to their oldest child's growing up and to the consequences for the family of the mother's going to work and the father's becoming a student again. Of course this meant the changing of roles, a new distribution of tasks, all of which evoked feelings that had not been expressed by any family member. Although cooperation and understanding had been stressed and was surely necessary to accomplish these tasks, neither the adults nor the children had ever articulated their feelings regarding the double crisis (adolescence and shift of parental roles due to new circumstances). The bitterness and hurt had gone underground until it suddenly burst open in a spree of actions totally atypical for the adolescent who engaged in them and for the family itself. Her unenviable role (maybe assigned, maybe assumed) was to be the instrument through which the hidden had to become overt. The paper made it clear that the student "knew what had happened" and also what needed to be done. Yet, the family continued to do what they always had done, namely acting as if nothing had happened. In my comments on the paper I challenged their attempt to reestablish the status quo. I do not know whether my ideas were accepted or put into action.

As the class draws to a close, the teaching-learning process moves from the content of family therapy, the statement of goals, the ending with families, some restatement of basic concepts and some quick attempt to fill some salient gaps in the teaching, to the students themselves as individuals and as a group. The talk moves to their ending. There is some expression of excitement and relief about the ending of the long and arduous process of school. They are relieved "to be done with it", to have achieved so important a goal, to get rid of all the work and pressures and to enter a world of professional service. For many this prospect is anxiety arousing as if what they have done thus far was a prelude to the "real thing". They are keenly aware that whatever the pressures on students, they had some protection which they now will have to give up. There is sadness intermingled with joy for the loss of comradeship among students, the loss of the total experience of learning and becoming; the opportunities found and those that were missed; for what was gotten and will be forever implanted as well as for what has not happened and will never be. Some of these feelings and thoughts are expressed, others are implied. Yet, all of them are connected with US, OUR class, OUR experience, OUR learning.

There comes a moment in the final class when words can no longer do justice to what is felt. So, at times but by no means always, I introduce the playing out of a scene which has to do with separation. I sometimes suggest that it may be a chance for those who thus far have not overtly participated to do just that. In other words, to change their pattern. In one class, we never got to the role playing since one female student became extremely upset at the memory of the child she had lost through death. All we as a group could do was to be with her around her pain.

The three incidents which I will next describe took place during the final session of three different classes. In one, a young woman replayed the scene when her parents and her younger brother brought her

169

to the college she was supposed to attend. An obviously loving family, it was not easy for them to part. I asked her to sculpt the last few moments before the actual parting took place. The student positioned her mother, who looked upset and was close to her, somewhat further away her father; his position did not make it clear whether or not he wanted to leave (he stood close to the car). The kid brother busied himself. After a while the student turned somewhat abruptly away, and went to join the other students. After a moment, the family departed in the car. The youngest child was settling down in the back seat. The sequence and emotions aroused were obvious and readily expressed. However, before allowing this to take place, I suggested that the student leave the room and asked the "family members" to show their reactions as they might have been half an hour later. They complied: they pulled up at a restaurant and their serious mood changed to a more pleasant one. Then I asked the student to come back and tell what she imagined her family had done after the leave-taking. As one could expect, she imagined continued sadness on the part of her folks. It is hard to get rid of images, especially those of emotionally charged moments. The person who leaves (or is being left) is not part of the ordinary stream of life and therefore, is often "stuck" with the stationary picture of his past. In this scene nothing dramatic had happened, a commonplace sadness familiar to most of us, yet something new was learned by the students in this last hour of their class: the concept of internalized images.

Another student, a refugee of the Nazi era, had spent many Summers in a Summer home (part of a Summer colony) next to a beautiful lake. She, her husband and their son had loved these Summers, but she herself was particularly attached to the landscape. One Summer, a real estate company bought all the land so that the homes had to be evacuated on the final day of Summer. The scene took place during the last hour prior to their leaving. The student sculpted herself standing in front of the house looking intently towards the lake and hills beyond it; behind her she arranged the rest of the students as the other families stood. They were busy with last minute preparations. Her husband stood close to her, facing the lake while their child was turning to the other families. Then, slowly and hesitantly, she went towards the "lake" (i.e., the window) without

170

words. She looked so lost that her husband followed
her and held her close (she said later that this is
what her real husband had done). Both stood this
way for some time. Only when their little boy came
towards them did she turn around abruptly and walk in
the other direction.

In another class, a silent student sculpted the
following scene[1]. She was five years old, living
with a man and a woman, the only parents she knew
and loved, when suddenly her "father" told her to
dress in her Sunday best, and her "mother" packed her
suitcase. She saw him turn his face, tears running
down his cheek. She did not understand. Her "mother"
took her hand and they went by trolley car to a house
which seemed vaguely familiar. They entered the
house and there was a young woman and other people
the child did not know. "This is your mother", said
the "mother". With this she left abruptly. The
child stood motionless, the suitcase next to her,
frozen. I do not believe that I or any other member
of the class will ever forget the pain of this scene.
Without any exchange of words, we recalled the student's rigid silence during all these weeks.

One can truly add nothing to such experiences.
This is how this book must end. I am left with the
realization that undertaking to write about the experiences of teaching is by no means the same as the
experience itself.

REFERENCE

1. Schulman, G.L., "Teaching Family Therapy to
    Social Work Students" in Social Casework, July
    1976.

BIBLIOGRAPHY

Course:

FAMILY ASSESSMENT AND TREATMENT

Students are told to keep this Bibliography
for later reference - they are not expected
to read all the books and articles, except
those required and those of special interest
to them

BOOKS

*Ackerman, N.W., Treating the Troubled Family,
  New York:Basic Books, 1966.

*Andolfi, M., Family Therapy, An Interactional Ap-
  proach, New York:Plenum Press, 1979.

 Boszormenyi-Nagy, I.and Frame, J.L.(eds.), Inten-
  sive Family Therapy: Theoretical and Practical
  Aspects, New York:Hoeber Medical Division, Harper
  & Row, 1965, chapters 2, 3, 5, 6, 10.

 Boszormenyi-Nagy, I., Invisible Loyalties, New York:
  Hoeber Medical Division, Harper & Row, 1973.

*Carter, E.A. and McGoldrick, M., The Family Life
  Cycle, New York:Gardner Press, Inc.,1980, p.174.

**Fitzpatrick, J.P., Puerto Rican America - The Mean-
  ing of Migration to the Mainland, Englewood Cliffs,
  N.J.:Prentice Hall, 1971.

*Guerin, P.J.,Jr., Family Therapy, New York:Halsted
  Press Division of John Wiley & Sons, 1976.

*Haley, J. (ed.), Changing Families, New York:Grune
  & Stratton, 1971.

**Haley, J., Leaving Home, New York:McGraw-Hill Book
  Co., 1980. (Recommended reading for those interested in enabling adolescents and young adults to
  separate from family of origin).

 Haley, J., Problem Solving Therapy, San Francisco:
  Jossey-Bass, Behavioral Science Series, 1976.

---

*Required Reading
**Special Interest Reading

BOOKS (ctd.)

*Hoffman, L., Foundations of Family Therapy, New York: Basic Books, 1981. .

**Jones, S.L., Family Therapy, a comparison of approaches, Bowie, Md.:Robert J. Brady Co., 1981.

Kaufman, E. and Kaufman, P.N.(eds.), Family Therapy of Drug and Alcohol Abuse, New York:Gardner Press, Inc., 1979.

**Madanes, C., Strategic Family Therapy, San Francisco: Jossey-Bass Behavioral Science Series, 1981.

*Minuchin, S., Families and Family Therapy,Cambridge: Harvard University Press, 1974.

**Minuchin, S., Montalvo, B. et al (eds.), Families of the Slums, New York:Basic Books, 1971.

*Minuchin, S., Fishman, Ch.H., Family Therapy Techniques, Cambridge:Harvard University Press, 1981.

Napier, A.Y. with Whitaker, C.S.,The Family Crucicle, New York:Harper & Row, 1978,

**Olivero, C.G., Study of the Initial Involvement in the Social Services by the Puerto Rican Migrants in Philadelphia, New York:Vantage Press, 1973,

Paolino, T.J.,Jr. and McCrady, B.S., Marriage and Marital Therapy, Psychoanalytic Behavior and Systems Perspectives, New York:Brunner/Mazel, 1978.

Papp. P. (ed.), Family Therapy, Full Length Case Studies, New York:Gardner Press, 1977.

*Satir, V., Conjoint Family Therapy, Palo Alto,Cal.: Science and Behavior Books, 1967,

**Selvini Palazzoli, M., Paradox and Counterparadox, New York:Jason Aronson, 1978.

*Watzlawick, P. et al, Change: Principles of Problem Formation and Problem Resolution, N.Y.:Norton,1974.

Zuk, G. and Boszormenyi-Nagy, I. (eds.), Family Therapy and Disturbed Families, Palo Alto, Calif: Science and Behavior Books, 1967.

JOURNALS

American Journal of Orthopsychiatry

Jan. 1979 Abarbanel, A., "Shared Parenting after Separation and Divorce: A Study of Joint Custody".
Grief, J.B., "Fathers, Children and Joint Custody".

174

Am.J.of Orthopsychiatry (ctd.)

Jan. 1979   Ransom, J.W. et al, "A Stepfamily in Form-
  (ctd.)   ation".

Family Process

Mar. 1965   Jackson, D.D., "The Study of the Family".

Sep. 1966   *Curry, A.E., "The Family Therapy Situation
            as a System".

Mar. 1967   Jensen, G. et al "Family Mourning Process".

            Machatka, P. et al, "Incest as a Family
            Affair".

Mar. 1969   Charny, I.W. et al,"Marital Love and Hate".

            Mosher, L.R., "Schizophrenogenic Communi-
            cation and Family Therapy".

Sep. 1969   Beels, C.C. and Ferber, A., "Family Ther-
            apy: A View".

            **Hoffman, L. and Long, L., "A Systems Di-
            lemma".

            *Speck, R.V. et al, "Network Therapy: A
            Developing Concept".

Mar. 1970   Kardener, S.H., "Convergent Internal Se-
            curity Systems".

            Meissner, W.W., "Sibling Relations in the
            Schizophrenic Family".

Sep. 1970   *Speer, D., "Family Systems: Morphostasis
            and Morphogenesis, or is Homeostasis
            enough?".

Dec. 1970   *Ackerman, N.W., "Child Participation in
            Family Therapy".

Sep. 1971   *Auerswald, E.H., "Families, Change and the
            Ecological Perspective".

Dec. 1971   Schefler, A.E., "Living Space in an Urban
            Ghetto".

            Stierlin, H. et al, "Parental Perceptions
            of Separating Children".

Mar. 1972   Olson, D.H., "Empirical Unbinding the
            Double Bind: Review of Research and Con-
            ceptual Reformulations".

            *Simon, R.M., Sculpting the Family".

Family Process (ctd.)

June 1972   Kaffman, M., "Family Conflict in the Psy-
            chopathology of the Kibbutz Child".

            Osman, S., "My Stepfather is a She".

            Umbarger, C., "The Paraprofessional and
            Family Therapy".

Sep. 1972 *Wertheim, E.S., "Family Unit Therapy and
            the Science of Typology of Family Systems".

Mar. 1973 *Aponte, H., Hoffman, L., "The Open Door: A
            Structural Approach to a Family with an
            Anorectic Child".

June 1973 *Papp, P. et al, "Family Sculpting in Pre-
            ventive Work with Well Families".

           *Solomon, M.A., "A Developmental, Conceptu-
            al Premise for Family Therapy".

           *Stierlin, H., "Group Fantasies and Family
            Myths - Some Theoretical and Practical
            Aspects".

Sep. 1973   Camp, H., "Structural Family Therapy: An
            Oursider's Perspective".

Dec. 1973   Montalvo, B., "Aspects of Live Supervision"
            (for advanced students).

            Slipp, S., "The Symbiotic Survival Pattern:
            A Relational Theory of Schizophrenia".

Mar. 1974   Leichter, E. and Schulman, G., "Multi-
            Family Group Therapy: A Multidimensional
            Approach" (advanced).

June 1974   Spark, M., "Grandparents and Intergenera-
            tional Family Therapy".

           *Weakland, J. et al, "Brief Therapy:
            Focused Problem Resolution".

Sep. 1974 *Boyd, E. et al, "Teaching Interpersonal
            Communication to Troubled Families".

Dec. 1974   Byng-Hall, J. and Bruggen, P., "Family Ad-
            mission Decisions as a Therapeutic Tool"
            (especially advised for those working in
            mental institutions).

            Selvini Palazzoli, M. et al, "The Treatment
            of Children through Brief Therapy of their
            Parents".

Family Process (ctd.)

Dec. 1974   Slipp, S. et al, "Factors Associated with Engagement in Family Therapy" (research).

Mar. 1975   Sluzki, C.E., "The Coalitionary Process in Initiating Family Therapy".

Whitaker, C.A., "Psychotherapy of the Absurd".

June 1975   Gordon, J.S., "Working with Runaways and Their Families: How the SAJA Community does it".

Reuveni, U., "Network Intervention with a Family in Crisis".

Sep. 1975   *Bark, S. et al, "Sisterhood-Brotherhood is Powerful: Sibling Sub-systems and Family Therapy" (advanced).

Peel, E., "'Normal' Sex Roles: An Historical Analysis".

*Wertheim, E.S., "The Science and Typology of Family Systems II. Further Theoretical and Practical Considerations" (advanced).

Mar. 1976   Cromwell, R.E. et al, "Tools and Techniques for Diagnosis in Marital and Family Therapy" (advanced).

Karpel, M., "Individuation: From Fusion to Dialogue".

Steinglass, P., Experimenting with Family Treatment Approaches to Alcoholism, 1950-1975: A Review".

Sep. 1976   Aponte, H., "The Family School Interview: An Eco-structural Approach".

*Klugman, J., "Enmeshment and Fusion".

Noone, R.J. and Reddig, R.L., "Case Studies in the Family Treatment of Drug Abuse".

Mar. 1977   Steinglass, P., Davis, D.I. and Berenson, D., "Observations of Conjointly Hospitalized 'Alcoholic Couples' during Sobriety and Intoxication".

June 1977   "Drug Abuse in the Family" (entire issue)

Sep. 1977   Goldman, J. et al, "Family Therapy After the Divorce: Developing a Strategy".

Family Process (ctd.)

Sep. 1977   Strolnick, A.H., "Multiple Family Group
            Therapy: A Review of the Literature".

Dec. 1977   Berkowitz, D., "On the Reclaiming of Denied
            Affects in Family Therapy".

            Caille, P. et al, "A Systems Theory Ap-
            proach to a Case of Anorexia Nervosa"
            (advanced).

            Kressel, K. et al, "Divorce Therapy: An
            In-depth Survey of Therapists' Views".

            Selvini Palazzoli, M. et al, "Family Rit-
            uals a Powerful Tool in Family Therapy"
            (advanced).

Jan. 1978   Bell, J.E., "Family Context Therapy: A
            Model for Family Change".

            Zuk, G., "A Therapist's Perspective on
            Jewish Family Values".

Mar. 1978   Gurman, A.S., "Deterioration in Marital and
            Family Therapy: Empirical, Clinical and
            Conceptual Issues" (advanced, research).

            Jefferson, C., "Some Notes on the Use of
            Family Sculpture in Therapy".

June 1978   Hare-Mustin, P.T., "A Feminist Approach to
            Family Therapy".

June 1979**Keeney, B.P., "Ecosystemic Epistemology:
            An Alternate Paradigm for Diagnosis".

            Richman, J., "The Family Therapy of At-
            tempted Suicide".

            Walker, K., "Dissolution and Reconstruction
            of Family Boundaries".

            Weisman, M., "Jealousy: Systemic, Problem-
            solving Therapy with Couples".

Sep. 1979   White, M., "Structural and Strategic Ap-
            proaches to Psychosomatic Families".

Dec. 1979   Sluzki, C.E., "Migration and Family Con-
            flict".

Mar. 1980   Bergman, J.S., "The Use of Paradox in a
            Community Home for the Chronically Dis-
            turbed and Retarded".

            *Papp, P., "The Greek Chorus and Other Tech-
            niques of Family Therapy".

178

Family Process (ctd.)

Mar. 1980 *Selvini Palazzoli, M., Boscolo, L. et al, "Hypothesizing - Circularity - Neutrality: Three Guidelines for the Conductor of the Session".

June 1980 Kreston, J-A. and Sepko, C., "The Problem of Fusion in the Lesbian Relationship" (advanced).

Madanes, C., "The Prevention of Rehospitalization of Adolescents and Young Adults".

Sep. 1980**Saposnek, D.T., "Aikido: A Model for Brief Strategic Therapy".

Steinglass, P., "A Life History Model of the Alcoholic Family" (advanced).

Dec. 1980**Dell, P.F. "Researching the Family Theories of Schizophrenics: an exercise in epistomological confusion".

Teisman, M.W., "Convening Strategies in Family Therapy".

International Journal of Family Therapy

Summer'80**Madanes, C., "Marital Therapy when a Symptom is Presented by a Spouse".

Summer'81 *Schulman, G.L., "Divorce, Single Parenthood and Stepfamilies: Structural Implications of these Transitions".

International Journl of Group Psychotherapy

Oct. 1970 MacGregor, R., "Group and Family Therapy: Moving into the Present and Letting Go of the Past".

Apr. 1978 Cohen, C.I. et al, "A Further Application of Balance Theory to Multiple Family Therapy".

Lansky, M.R. et al, "Multiple Family Groups as Aftercare".

Wellisch, David K. et al,"Management of Family, Emotion, Stress: Family Group Therapy in a Private Oncology Practice".

Journal of Group Psychoanalysis and Process

Summer'69 *Schulman, G.L., "Family Intake to Counter Family Fragmentation".

Journal of Jewish Communal Service

Summer'75 *Schulman, G.L., "The Single-Parent Family".

Journal of Marital and Family Therapy
  (formerly Journal of Marriage and Family Counseling)

Jan. 1975 Foley, V.D., "Family Therapy with Black Disadvantaged Families".

           Framo, J.L., "Personal Reflections of a Family Therapist".

           Haley, J., "Why a Mental Health Clinic Should Avoid Family Therapy".

July 1975 Bochus, F., "A Systems Approach to Marital Process".

           Humphrey, F.G., "Changing Roles for Women: Implications for Marriage Counselors".

Apr. 1976 *Feldman, L.B., "Goals of Family Therapy".

July 1977 Buckland, C.M., "An Educational Model of Family Consultation".

Jan. 1978 Andolfi, M., "A Structural Approach to a Family with an Encopretic Child".

           Napier, A.Y., "The Rejection-Intrusion Pattern: A Central Family Dynamic".

Apr. 1978 Constantine, L., "Family Sculpture and Relationship Mapping Techniques".

July 1978 Levant, R.F., "Family Therapy: A Client Centered Approach".

           Selvini Palazzoli, M.et al, "A Ritualized Prescription in Family Therapy: Odd Days and Evenings".

           White, S.L., "Family Theory According to the Cambridge Model".

           Wile, D.B., "Is a Confrontational Tone Necessary in Conjoint Therapy?".

Jan. 1979 Ackerman, B.L., "Relational Paradox: Towards a Language of Interactional Sequences". (advanced)

J. of Marital and Family Therapy (ctd.)

Jan. 1979   Farley, J., "Family separation - Individ-
(ctd.)   ual Tolerance - A Developmental Concept-
             ualization of Nuclear Family". (advanced)

             Gurman, A.S., "Dimensions of Marital Ther-
             apy: A Comparative Analysis". (advanced
             and research)

             Kaslow, F.W. and Cooper, B., "Family Ther-
             apy with the Learning Disabled Child and
             His/Her Family".

Apr. 1979   Hare-Mustin, R.T., "Family Therapy Follow-
             ing the Death of a Child".

             Kleinman, J. et al, "Common Development
             Tasks in Forming Reconstituted Families".

             Solomon, M.A. and Hersch, L.B., "Death in
             the Family: Implications for Family De-
             velopment".

Jan. 1980   Davis, D.I., "Alcoholics Anonymous and
             Family Therapy".

Social Casework

Mar. 1968 *Schulman, G.L. and Leichter, E., "The Pre-
             vention of Family Breakup".

Feb. 1970 *Hallowitz, D., "The Problem-Solving Com-
             ponent in Family Therapy".

June 1970 *McKinney, G.E., "Adapting Family Therapy
             to Multi-Deficit Families".

Feb. 1971   Irving, H.H., "Relationships Between Mar-
             ried Couples and their Parents".

Mar. 1972 *Schulman, G.L., "Myths That Intrude on the
             Adaptation of the Stepfamily".

Jan. 1973 *Leader, A.L., "Family Therapy for Di-
             vorced Fathers and Others Out of the
             Home".

             Thale, Th., "Effect of Medication on the
             Caseworker-Client Relationship".

Oct. 1973 *Schulman, G.L., "Treatment of Intergenera-
             tional Pathology".

Jan. 1974   Boisvert, M.J., "Behavior Shaping as an
             Alternative to Psycho-Therapy".
             Davies, M., The Assessment of Environment
             in Social Work Research".

181

Social Casework (ctd.)

Apr. 1974 Mostwin, D., "Multidimensional Model of Working with the Family".

June 1974 Lang, J., "Planned Short-Term Treatment in a Family Agency".

Apr. 1975 *Rosenberg, B., "Planned Short-Term Treatment in Developmental Crises".

July 1975 Greenberg, L.I., "Therapeutic Grief Work with Children".

Leader, A.L., "The Place of In-Laws in Marital Relationships".

Feb. 1976 Duhl, F.J., "Changing Sex Roles - Concepts, Values, Tasks".

Lipman-Blumen, J., "The Implications for Family Structure of Changing Sex Roles".

May 1976 Levanda, D.I., "Family Theory as a Necessary Component of Family Therapy".

July 1976 Schulman, G.L., "Teaching Family Therapy to Social Work Students".

Oct. 1976 *Halleck, S.R., "Family Therapy and Social Change".

Nov. 1976 Zimmerman, S., "The Family and its Relevance for Social Policy".

Dec. 1976 Leader, A.L., "Denied Dependency in Family Therapy".

Feb. 1977 Orcutt, B.A., "Family Treatment of Poverty Level Families".

Mar. 1978 Leader, A.L., "Intergenerational Separation Anxiety in Family Therapy".

Oct. 1978 Hartman, A., "Diagrammatic Assessment of Family Relationships".

Social Work

May 1979 *Jacobson, D.S., "Stepfamilies: Myths and Realities".

Mendes, H.A., "Single Parent Families: A Typology of Life Styles".